EASY PIANO

SONGS OF THE 40's

THE DECADE S

ISBN 0-7935-2668-X

7777 W. BLUEMOUND RD. P.O. BOX 13819 MILWAUKEE, WI 53213

SONGS OF THE 40's

THE DECADE SERIES

The Forties

by Stanley Green

Pearl Harbor

*A*t first they called it the Phony War, when it seemed as if the French and German armies would be forever stalemated on opposite sides of the Maginot Line. But four months into the new decade, the Second World War erupted in all its fury with a staggering succession of pulverizing Nazi blitzkriegs. Denmark fell in four hours. Norway in thirty-two days. Holland in five days. Belgium in eighteen. After seven of Hitler's columns pushed their way into France, the best that British and French forces could do was to escape annihilation through their heroic rescue at Dunkirk. With Italy now in the war on the side of its Axis partner, France was forced into a humiliating surrender in a railroad carriage in the forest of Compiegne. British Prime Minister Winston Churchill rallied his island kingdom by offering nothing more than "blood, toil, tears, and sweat," as night after night the Luftwaffe bombarded the major cities of England. Then, inevitably, the war spread to eastern Europe when the tenuous alliance between Hitler and Stalin was shattered by Germany's invasion of the Soviet Union.

On this side of the Atlantic, President Franklin D. Roosevelt, now serving an unprecedented third term, declared an unlimited state of national emergency, arranged a lend-lease program to aid the beleaguered Allies, proclaimed the United States "the arsenal of democracy," and joined with Churchill in spelling out their peace aims in the Atlantic Charter. Nothing, however, could control events or stem the spreading carnage. On December 7, 1941 — a date, Roosevelt said, "which will live in infamy" — the Japanese struck at Pearl Harbor and the United States was at last officially in the conflict.

It wasn't long before Americans became familiar with the names of faraway places that only a few had ever heard of before — Bataan and Corregidor in the Philippines where Gen. Douglas MacArthur's men were forced to surrender...Sevastopol, where Russian defenders held out against the German juggernaut for eight months...

Harry S. Truman

Lidice, Czechoslovakia, where Nazis slaughtered an entire village...El Alamein and Tobruk, where British victories turned the tide against Field Marshal Erwin Rommel's Afrika Korps... Guadalcanel, the first Japanese island to be recaptured by American forces...Anzio, on the western Italian coast, where U.S. and British troops made their initial landings in Europe...Auschwitz, where 476,000 Hungarian Jews were sent to their death...Omaha Beach on the French Normandy coastline where, on "D-Day," Gen. Dwight D. Eisenhower's liberating armies met their fiercest resistance... Tacloban on the island of Leyte, where MacArthur waded ashore to begin the liberation of the Philippines...Iwo Jima, where Yanks wrested control from the Japanese and raised the stars and stripes atop Mt. Suribachi...Hiroshima and Nagasaki, where President Harry S. Truman, Roosevelt's successor, made the fateful decision to drop the atom bomb that brought the war to an end.

Iwo Jima

It is no flattery to give a friend a due character. for commendation is as much the duty of a

THE GREAT
Breakfast Table Paper
OF NEW ENGLAND

The Boston Post

TUESDAY FEBRUARY 20 1945 **

Established 1831.

SIXTEEN PAGES—TWO CENTS

Midnight Curfew on U. S. Night Spots

BYRNES' ORDER STARTS FEB. 26

Fuel-Saving Decree Hits Drinking Places, Dance Halls, Theatres for Sports

VINCENT GIRLS BUSY DURING DAY

Hold Rehearsals for Annual Show at Night Because Members Now Work From 9 to 5

YANKS WINNING BIG IWO BATTLE

30,000 Marines Conquering Island in Pacific War's Most Se—
Struggle----Japs, Holed Up in Thousands of Ca—
——outs Putting Up Furious Resista—

Reds Say Nazis Slew 4 Million In Polish Camp

Trumans Move to
On Eve of Victor

NEW YORK
Herald Tribune

THURSDAY, MAY 3, 1945

Berlin Falls; Hitler a
Killed Selves, R
Nazis Yield It.

THE MILWAUKEE JOURNAL

Monday, May 7, 1945

All Germans Surrender
to Three Major Alli

Official
in Sch

Spain Locks Up Laval for Allies;
Defied Franco Order to Get Out

Nazis in
Give Up W
A Million Men.

German Chiefs
Tell War's End

VICTORY EX

San Francisco Chro

SAN FRANCISCO, WEDNESDAY, AUGUST 15, 19

PEAC

NEW YORK
Herald Tribune

TUESDAY, MAY 8, 1945

V-E DAY
EDITION

oday Is V-E Day

—n, Churchill, Stalin to Proclaim War's E
—rmans Surrender at Eisenhower's Headqu

The Japs Give Up Unconditi
Allied Troops Told to Cease
Enemy Gets Orders for Sur

A City Goes Wild---
And Nobody Cares

Defeated Officers Will
Hirohito and

Like most wars, World War II produced its share of patriotic, inspirational, sentimental, and comic songs that still evoke memories of those tragic and courageous times. From England, "A Nightingale Sang in Berkeley Square" offered a measure of hope during the dark days of the Battle of Britain; "The Last Time I Saw Paris" was Jerome Kern and Oscar Hammerstein's tender recollection of the charms of the French capital in the days before the Nazi occupation; the haunting "Lili Marlene," though a German song, was soon adopted by British and American forces in North Africa; and "Saturday Night Is the Loneliest Night in the Week" was the lament of frustrated young women everywhere who were compelled to spend their weekends alone while their loved ones were serving their country.

Once the war was finally over, the leaders of this ravaged planet set about the difficult task of searching for ways to establish a lasting peace. In the summer of 1945, representatives of 46 nations met in San Francisco to sign the charter of the United Nations. Nazi war criminals were brought to justice at the Nuremberg trials. And the Marshall Plan — named for its sponsor, Secretary of State George C. Marshall — was approved by Congress to help rehabilitate the countries of Europe and Asia.

Other major events, both shocking and dramatic, were also occurring in the United States during the post-war years. The French liner Normandie burned and sank while tied up in New York harbor. In Boston, 491 people perished in the Cocoanut Grove fire. The House Un-American Activities Committee set up shop to ferret out Communists, and Whittaker Chambers accused State Department aide Alger Hiss of being a Soviet spy. The Forties also saw the biggest political upset in American history when Truman confounded the pollsters by beating Gov. Thomas E. Dewey in the Presidential election. For diversion from matters of state and weight, the "New Look" was emphasizing longer, fuller skirts; canasta became the latest card-game craze; people actually claimed to see flying saucers in the sky; and changes in home entertainment were being caused by two important developments — the boom in the popularity of television and the invention of the long-playing record.

V-J Day Parade

When the decade began, dance orchestras were still providing the chief means through which song hits were being made. The main difference was that the beat had slowed down noticeably since the heyday of the swing bands. Thus Sammy Kaye's Swing and Sway boys were more likely to sway than to swing such numbers as "The Old Lamplighter" and "Daddy." Harry James' luminous horn took on a mellower tone as it led the band in "I'm Beginning to See the Light" (co-composed by James and Duke Ellington). And Glenn Miller's orchestra was suitably ethereal as it brought back memories of "Polka Dots and Moonbeams." Occasionally, though, a jazzier, more uptempo beat would break through, notably in Miller's "Tuxedo Junction," Tommy Dorsey's "Opus One," and both Miller's and Benny Goodman's versions of "A String of Pearls."

One special sound that won favor throughout the Forties was that of Latin and Latin-type music. "The Breeze and I" was adapted from Cuban composer Ernesto Lecuona's "Andalucia, Suite Española" to become a hit single for Tommy Dorsey's older brother Jimmy, who also had success with the Spanish "Amapola." And another Cuban number, "Poinciana," became a top selling record in its lush treatment by David Rose and his Orchestra.

Frank Sinatra

But it was becoming abundantly clear that the days of the mass popularity of big bands were numbered. Not only did wartime travel restrictions make it difficult for them to tour the country, the drafting of many musicians into the services helped bring about a sharp reduction in available personnel. Even in the early Forties, their place in the musical spotlight was being shared by the vocalists — whether singly or in groups — who would become the dominant attraction by the decade's end. During the war years, no performers were more closely identified with the music of the period than the harmonizing Andrews Sisters. One of their catchiest hits, "Boogie Woogie Bugle Boy," even managed to combine the sound of boogie woogie (a rumbling figured-bass pattern associated with honky-tonk pianos) with an up-to-date lyric about an irrepressible GI bugler.

The Andrews Sisters

"Pal Joey"

"Oklahoma!"

Rodgers & Hammerstein

Looming even larger on the musical scene was a hollow-cheeked, ex-band singer named Frank Sinatra who, in 1943, caused 30,000 bobby soxers to riot in the streets during an engagement at New York's Paramount Theatre. Also attracting loyal fans were such singing sensations of the decade as Ella Fitzgerald ("Imagination"), the Mills Brothers ("I Don't Want to Set the World on Fire," "I'll Be Around," "Across the Alley from the Alamo"), Jo Stafford ("Candy"), Nat "King" Cole ("For Sentimental Reasons"), Dinah Shore ("Shoo-Fly Pie and Apple Pan Dowdy"), and Vaughn Monroe ("Ballerina").

"One Touch Of Venus"
Starring Mary Martin

"Kiss Me, Kate"

On Broadway, Richard Rodgers was acknowledged as the decade's most influential composer. With his first partner, lyricist Lorenz Hart, he wrote the score for the hard-edged, cynical *Pal Joey,* which gave Vivienne Segal the chance to sing "Bewitched" and Gene Kelly the chance to sing "I Could Write a Book." In 1943, Rodgers teamed with a new lyricist, Oscar Hammerstein II, to inaugurate a different form of musical theatre with their seminal production, *Oklahoma!* "Oh, What A Beautiful Mornin'," "People Will Say We're in Love," "The Surrey With the Fringe on Top," and "Oklahoma" were four of the standards in this landmark score, while "June Is Bustin' Out All Over" and "You'll Never Walk Alone" were among the gems in the second Rodgers and Hammerstein stage work, *Carousel.*

Other writers who graced Broadway with their songs were Harold Arlen and Johnny Mercer with *St. Louis Woman* ("Come Rain or Come Shine"), Burton Lane and E. Y. Harburg with *Finian's Rainbow* ("How Are Things in Glocca Morra?," "Old Devil Moon"), Cole Porter with his biggest hit, *Kiss Me, Kate* ("So in Love," "Wunderbar"), and Kurt Weill and Ogden Nash with *One Touch of Venus* ("Speak Low"), starring Mary Martin.

*M*otion pictures of the Forties also provided their share of musical pleasures. "When You Wish Upon a Star" (sung on the soundtrack by Cliff Edwards) was heard in Walt Disney's second full-length animated cartoon, *Pinocchio;* the canorous "I'll Remember April" turned up in — of all places — Abbott and Costello's *Ride 'Em, Cowboy;* and "You'd Be So Nice to Come Home To," by Cole Porter, was introduced in a long-forgotten movie called *Something to Shout About.* During the decade Bing Crosby maintained his position as the screen's number-one singing actor, appearing in twenty-two films including *Going My Way* ("Swinging on a Star") and *Road to Rio* ("But Beautiful"), the fifth of Crosby's seven "Road" shows with Bob Hope and Dorothy Lamour. Following their Broadway triumph *Oklahoma!,* Rodgers and Hammerstein contributed the songs to *State Fair,* another slice of rural Americana in which the swooping waltz "It's a Grand Night for Singing" was first sung. Al Jolson, once billed as "The World's Greatest Entertainer," enjoyed a comeback in the mid-Forties when his dubbed voice was heard coming out of the mouth of Larry Parks in *The Jolson Story.* Though the songs consisted of old favorites, there was one "new" ballad, "Anniversary Song," whose melody dated back sixty years to a Rumanian composition known as "Danube Waves." Also of foreign origin was Anton Karas's ominous, jangling theme from *The Third Man,* which was performed by the composer on a zither as background music for a drama of East-West espionage set in post-war Vienna.

*O*f course, people didn't need movies to remind them that international tensions still remained high in 1949. Still, there was some comfort to be derived from the fact that the decade ended not with a whimper (as did the Twenties), nor with a bang (as did the Thirties), but with an audible sigh of relief that no world-wide catastrophe seemed to be looming in the imminent future.

World Leaders

Franklin D. Roosevelt

Josef Stalin

Winston Churchill

Gen. Dwight D. Eisenhower

Gen. Douglas MacArthur

ACROSS THE ALLEY
FROM THE ALAMO

Words and Music by
JOE GREENE

Na - va - jo watched the la - zy skies _ And ver - y rare - ly did they ev - er
wash-in' their frijo - les in Duz and Lux, _ A pair of ver - y con - sci -

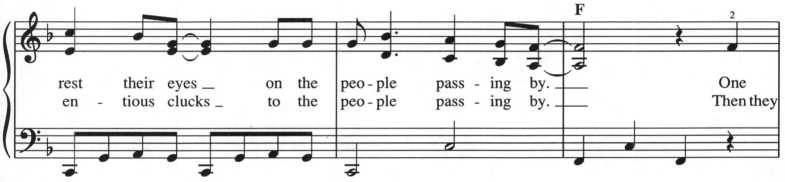

rest their eyes _ on the peo - ple pass - ing by. _ One
en - tious clucks _ to the peo - ple pass - ing by. _ Then they

day, they went a - walk- in,' _____ a - long the rail - road track, _
took this cheap va - ca - tion, _____ their shoes were pol - ished bright,

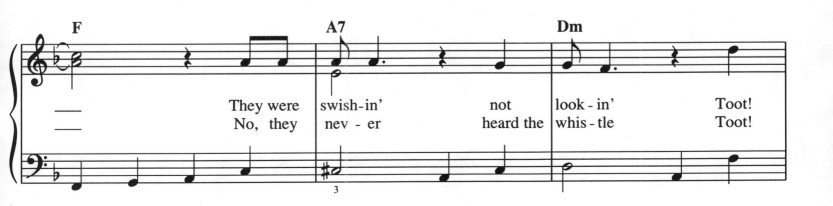

They were swish-in' not look - in' Toot!
No, they nev - er heard the whis - tle Toot!

14

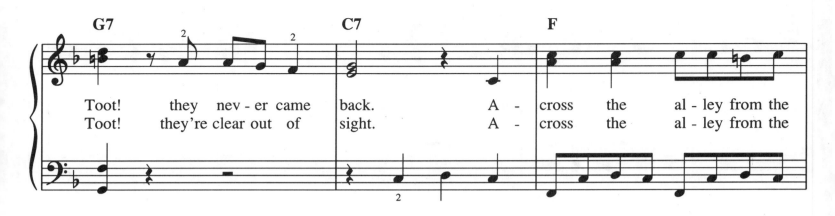

Toot! they nev - er came back. A - cross the al - ley from the
Toot! they're clear out of sight. A - cross the al - ley from the

Al - a - mo, __ When the sum - mer sun de-cides to set - tle low, __ A
Al - a - mo, __ When the star - light beams it's ten-der, ten - der glow, __ The

fly sings an In - di - an Hi - de - ho ____ to the peo - ple pass - ing by. __
beams go to sleep and there ain't no dough __ for the peo - ple pass - ing by. __

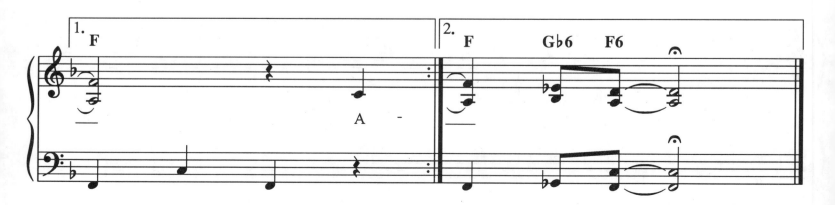

A -

AMAPOLA
(Pretty Little Poppy)

By JOSEPH M. LACALLE
New English Words by ALBERT GAMSE

A - ma - po - la, _____ my pret -ty lit - tle

pop - py, _____ You're like that love - ly flow'r so

sweet and heav- en - ly _____ Since I

found you, _____ My heart is wrapped a - round you _____

And lov - ing you, it seems to beat a

rhap - so - dy. _____ A - ma - po - la, _____

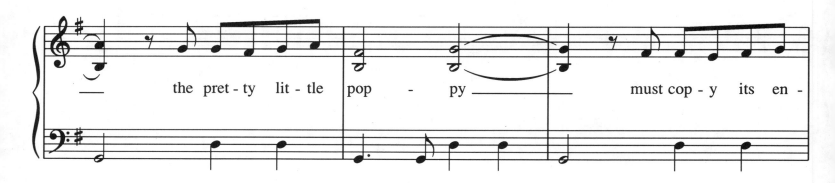

the pret - ty lit - tle pop - py _____ must cop - y its en -

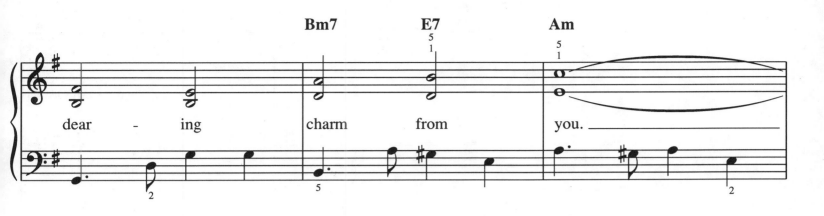

ANNIVERSARY SONG

By AL JOLSON
and SAUL CHAPLIN

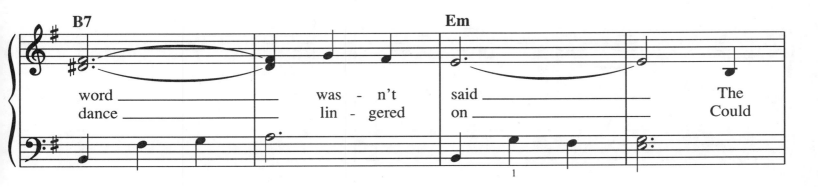

word _____ was - n't said _____ The
dance _____ lin - gered on _____ Could

world _____ was in bloom, _____ there were
we _____ but re - live _____ that sweet

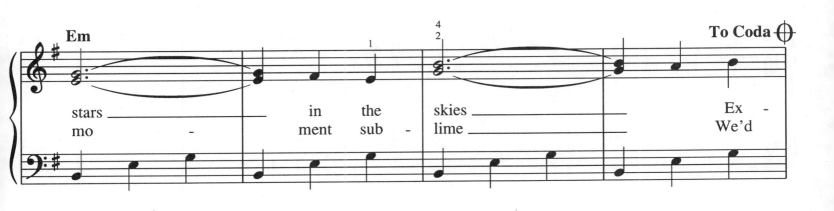

stars _____ in the skies _____ Ex -
mo - ment sub - lime _____ We'd

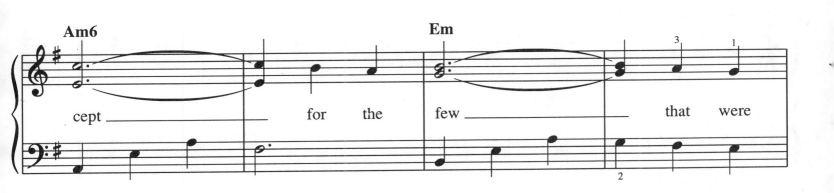

cept _____ for the few _____ that were

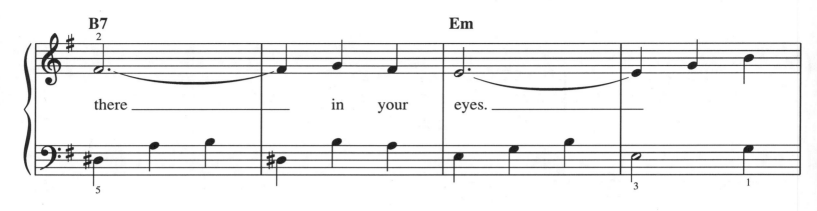

there _____ in your eyes. _____

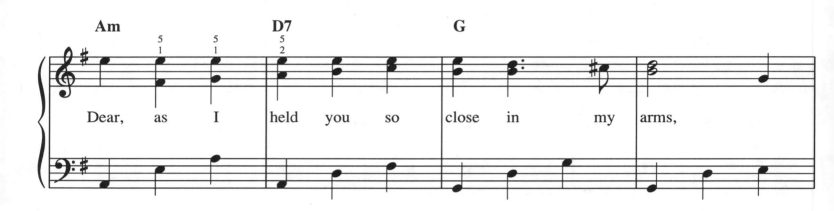

Dear, as I held you so close in my arms,

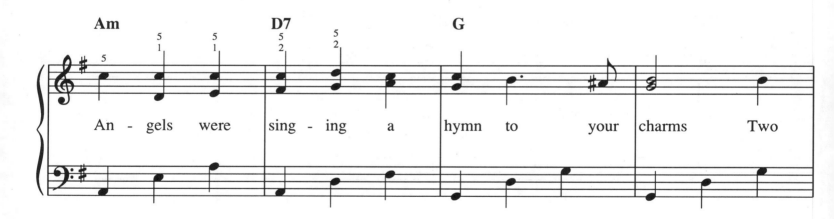

An - gels were sing - ing a hymn to your charms Two

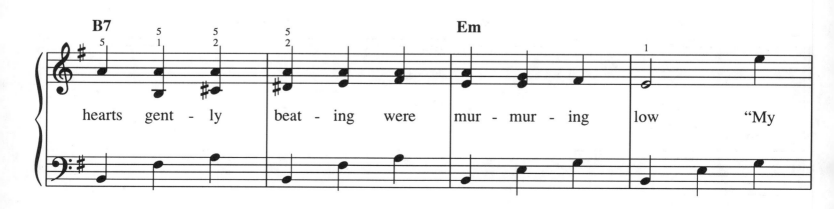

hearts gent - ly beat - ing were mur - mur - ing low "My

darling, I love you so."

The

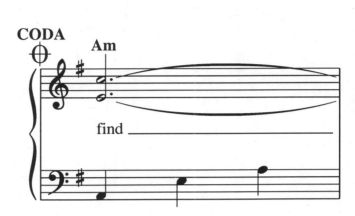

find

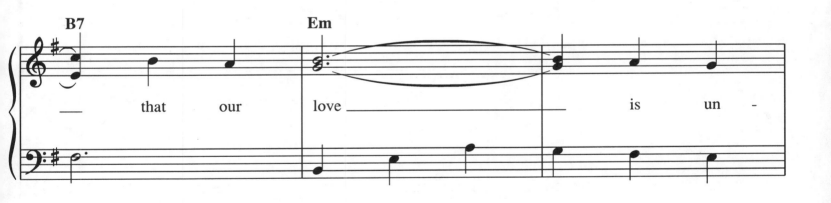

that our love is un-

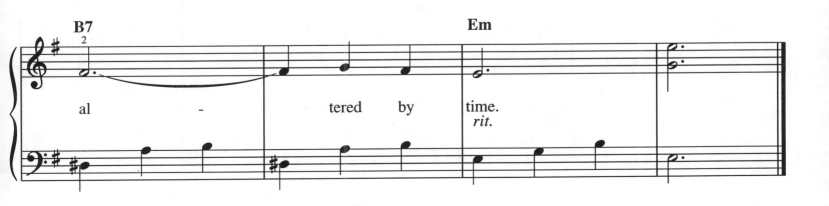

al - tered by time.

rit.

BEWITCHED
(From "PAL JOEY")

Words by LORENZ HART
Music by RICHARD RODGERS

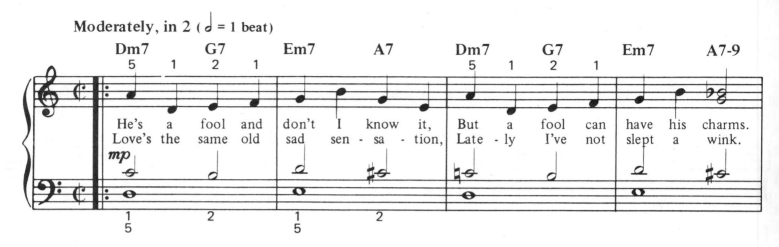

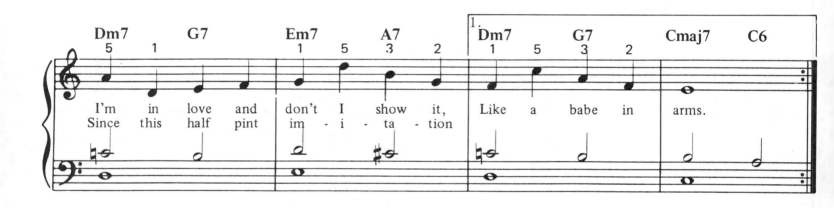

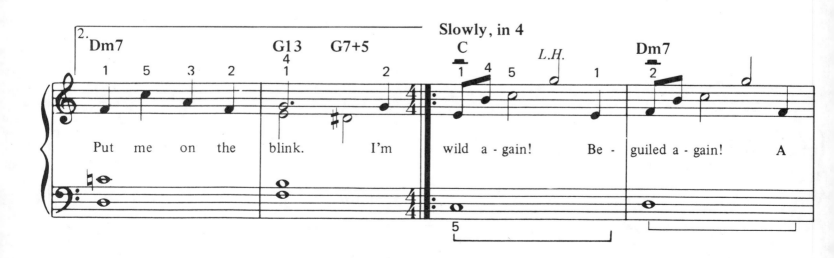

He is cold I a - gree. He can laugh but I love it Al-though the

laugh's on me. I'll sing to him, Each spring to him, And

long for the day when I'll cling to him, Be - witched, both-ered and be- wil - dered am

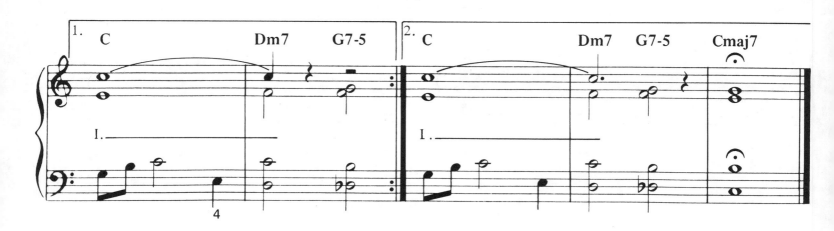

BLUEBERRY HILL

Words and Music by AL LEWIS,
LARRY STOCK and VINCENT ROSE

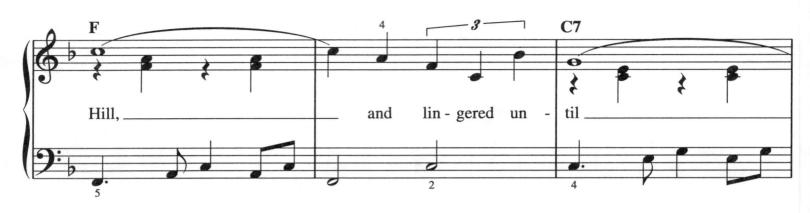

Hill, _____ and lin - gered un - til _____

_____ my dreams came true. _____ The wind in the

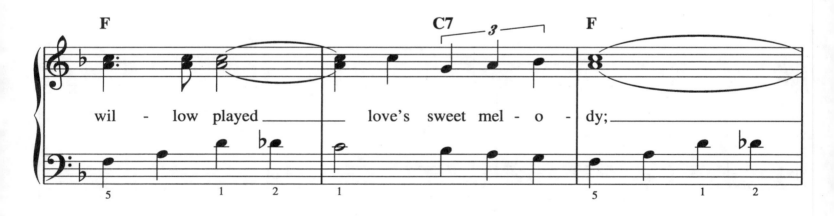

wil - low played _____ love's sweet mel - o - dy; _____

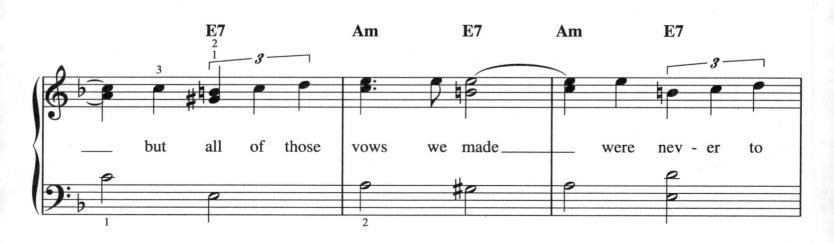

_____ but all of those vows we made _____ were nev - er to

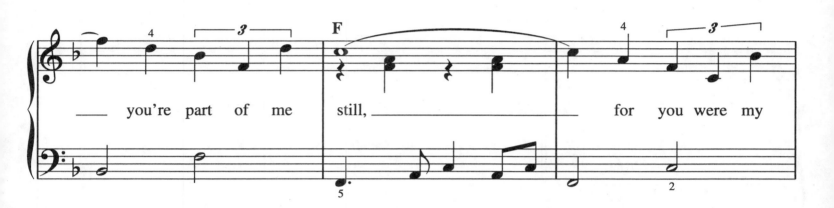

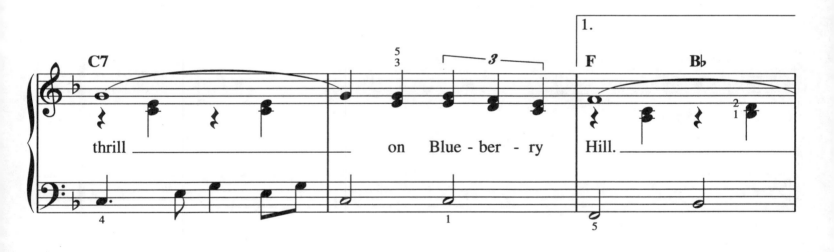

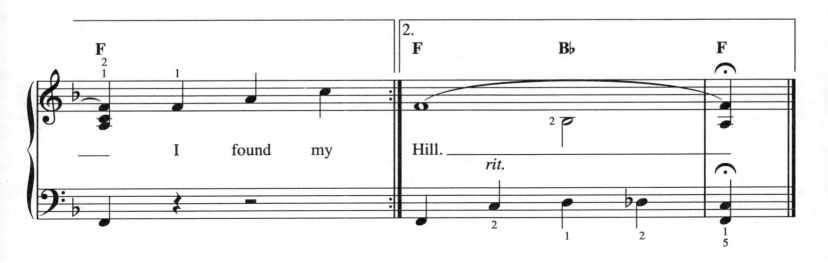

BOOGIE WOOGIE BUGLE BOY

Words and Music by DON RAYE
and HUGHIE PRINCE

MCA music publishing

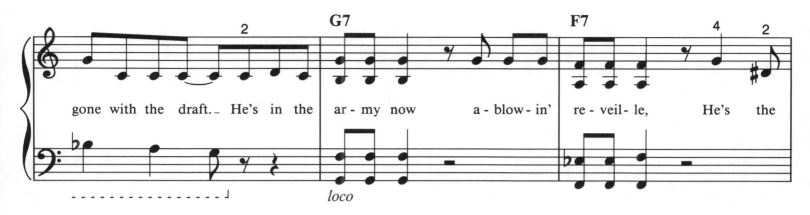

gone with the draft.— He's in the | ar - my now a - blow - in' re - veil - le, He's the

loco

Boo - gie Woo - gie Bu - gle Boy of Com - pa - ny "B.". — They

made him blow a bu - gle for his | Un - cle Sam, — It
puts the boys to sleep with "boo - gie" ev - 'ry night, — And

8va bassa

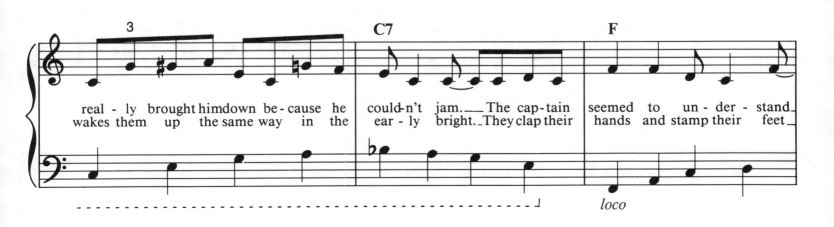

real - ly brought him down be - cause he | could - n't jam.— The cap - tain seemed to un - der - stand.—
wakes them up the same way in the ear - ly bright. They clap their hands and stamp their feet.—

loco

Be - cause the next day the "cap" — went out and
Be - cause they know how he plays — when some - one

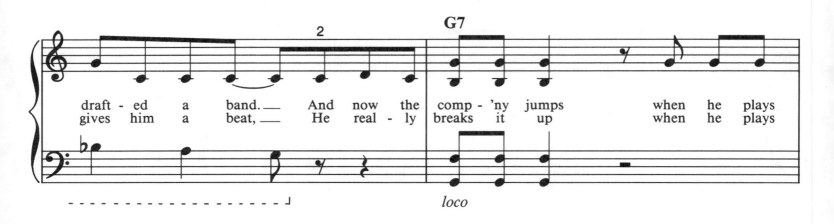

draft - ed a band.— And now the comp - 'ny jumps when he plays
gives him a beat, — He real - ly breaks it up when he plays

loco

re - veil - le,⎱ He's the Boo - gie Woo - gie Bu - gle Boy of Com - pan - y "B." — A
re - veil - le,⎰

8va bassa -

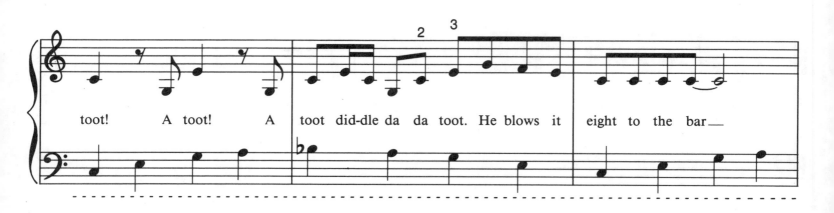

toot! A toot! A toot did - dle da da toot. He blows it eight to the bar—

in "boo - gie" rhy - thm. He can't blow a note un - less a

loco

bass and gui - tar___ is play - in' with 'im.___ He makes the

8va bassa -

comp - 'ny jump when he plays re - veil - le, He's the

loco

Boo - gie Woo - gie Bu - gle Boy of Com - pa - ny "B." _ He Com - pa - ny "B." _

8va bassa -

THE BREEZE AND I

Words by AL STILLMAN
Music by ERNESTO LECUONA

seemed con-stant as the moon end-ing in a strange mourn - ful

tune. _____ And all a - bout me they

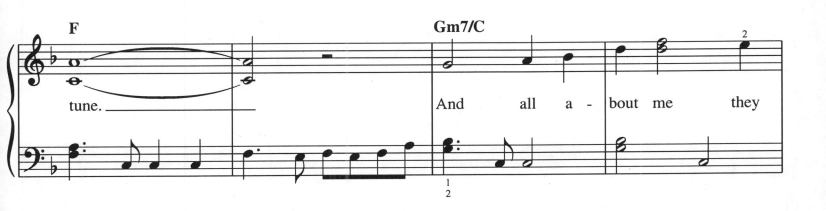

know you have de - part-ed with-out me and we won - der

why, _____ the breeze and I. _____

BUT BEAUTIFUL

Words by JOHNNY BURKE
Music by JIMMY VAN HEUSEN

take a chance and if you fall, you fall; And I'm

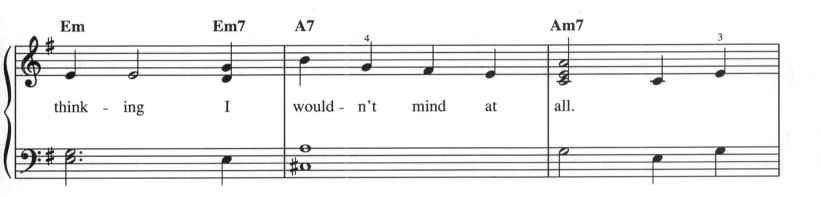

think - ing I would - n't mind at all.

Love is tear - ful or it's gay, it's a

prob - lem or it's play; It's a heart - ache eith - er

CANDY

Words and Music by MACK DAVID,
JOAN WHITNEY and ALEX KRAMER

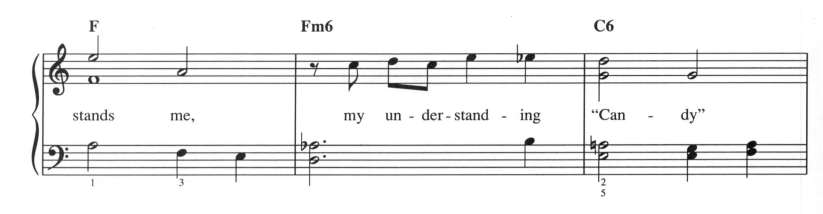

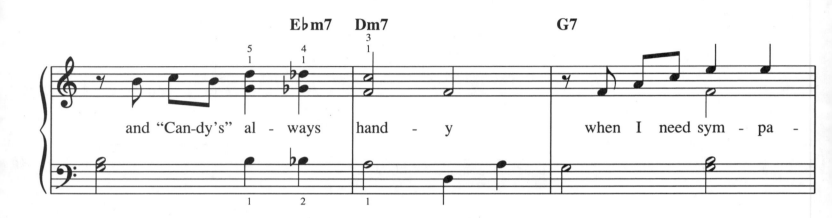

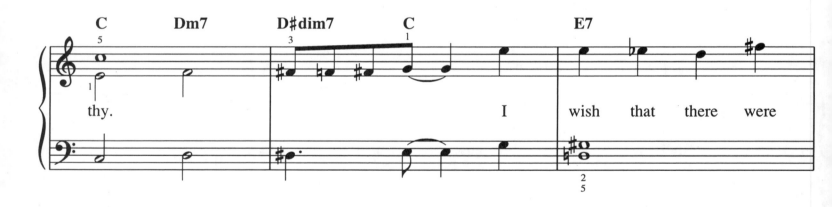

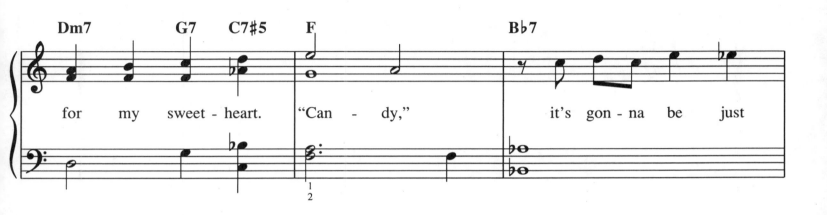

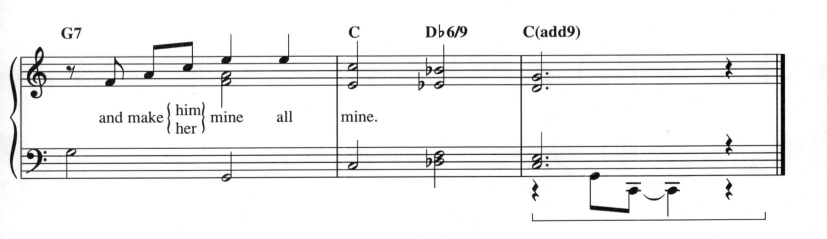

CRUISING DOWN THE RIVER

Words and Music by EILY BEADELL
and NELL TOLLERTON

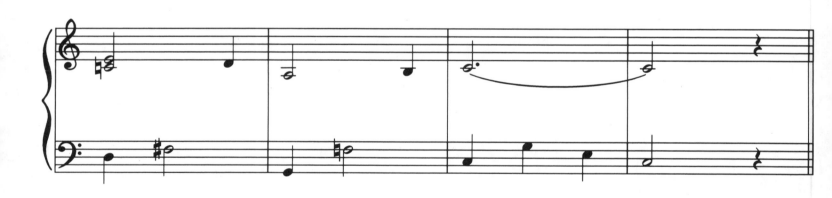

Cruis - ing down the riv - er, ___ on a

Sun - day aft - er - noon ____ with

one you love, the sun a - bove

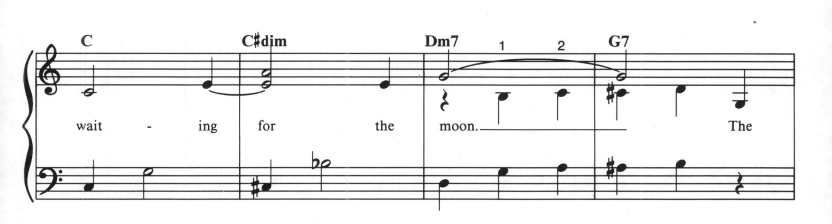

wait - ing for the moon. ____ The

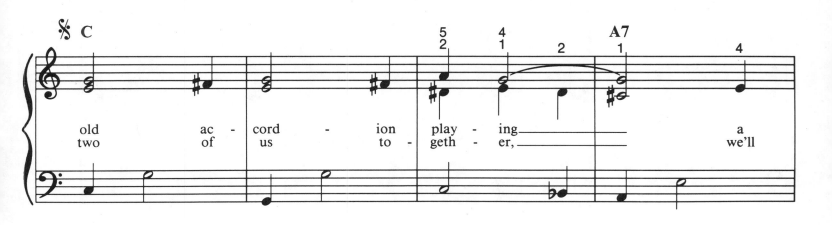

old ac - cord - ion play - ing ____ a
two of us to - geth - er, ____ we'll

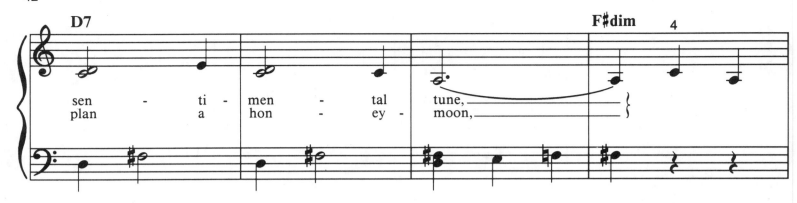

sen - ti - men - tal tune,_____
plan a hon - ey - moon,_____

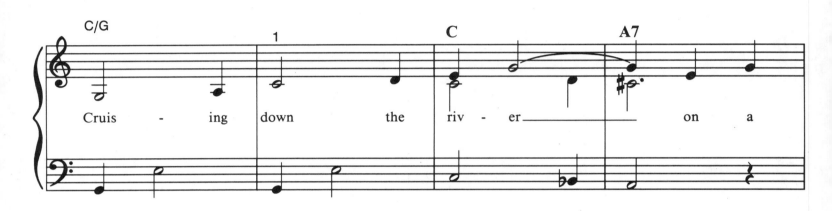

Cruis - ing down the riv - er_____ on a

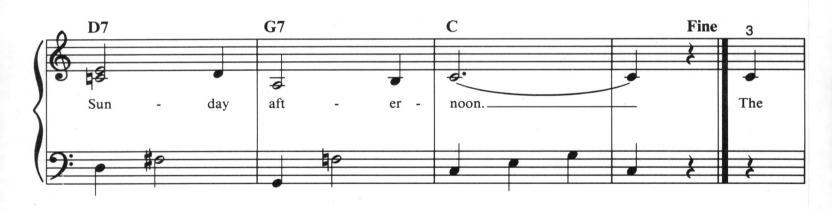

Sun - day aft - er - noon._____ The

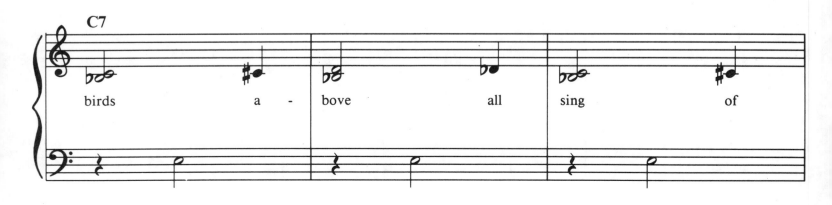

birds a - bove all sing of

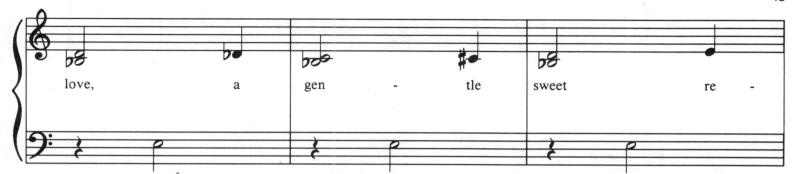

love, a gen - tle sweet re -

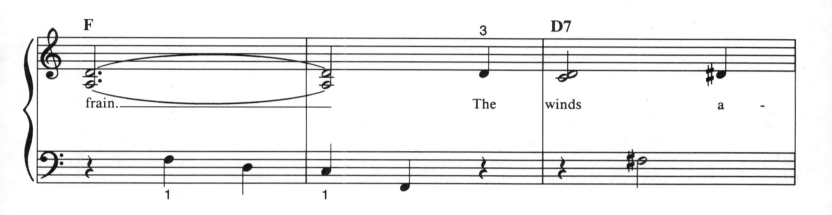

F **3** **D7**

frain. The winds a -

round all make a sound like

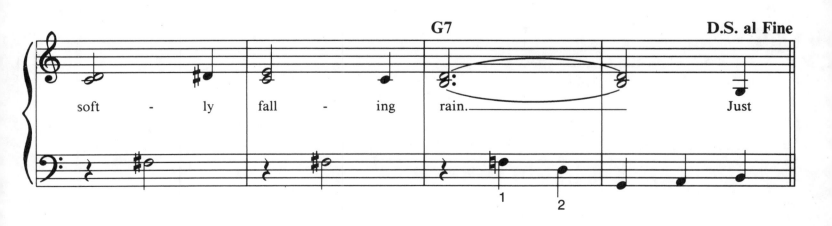

G7 **D.S. al Fine**

soft - ly fall - ing rain. Just

COME RAIN OR COME SHINE

(From "ST. LOUIS WOMAN")

Words by JOHNNY MERCER
Music by HAROLD ARLEN

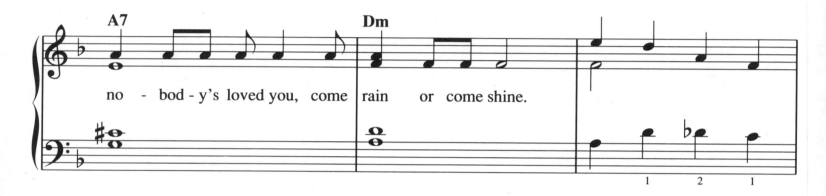

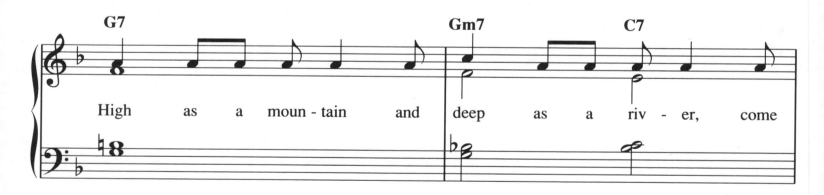

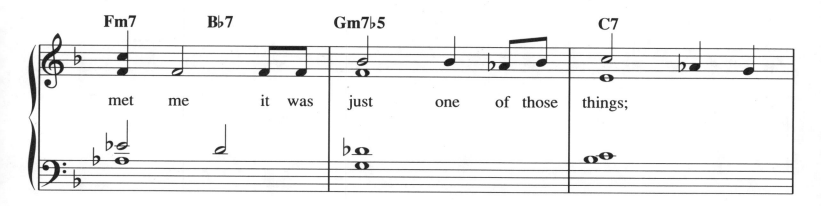

met me it was just one of those things;

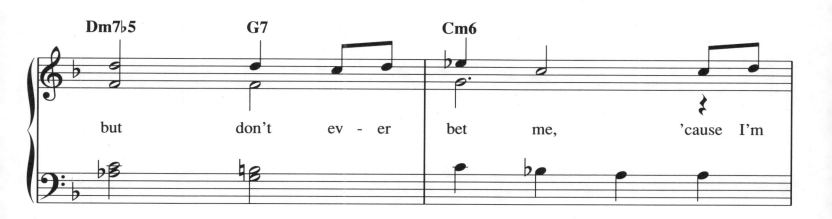

but don't ev - er bet me, 'cause I'm

gon - na be true if you let me. You're gon - na love me like

no - bod - y's loved me come rain or come shine.

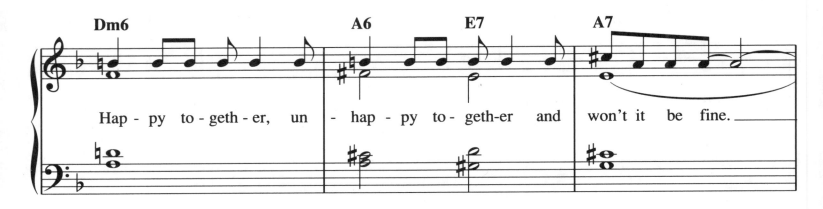

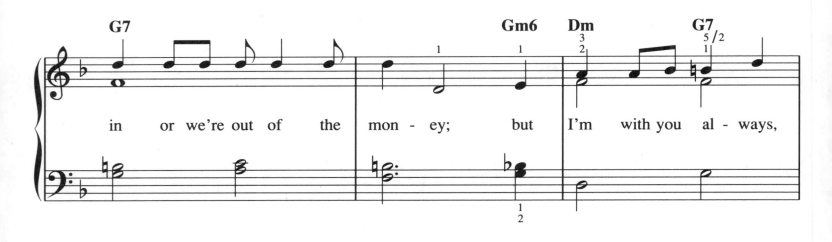

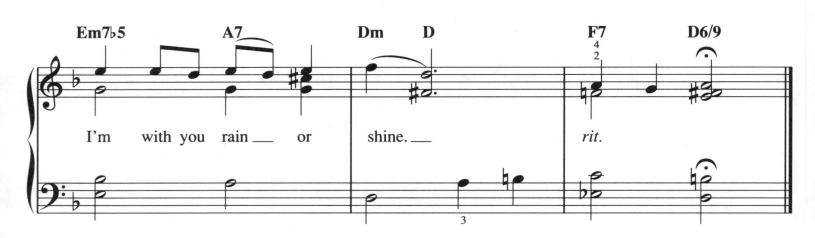

DADDY

Words and Music by
BOB TROUP

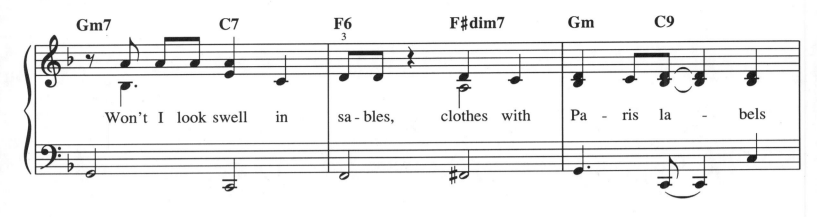

Won't I look swell in sa - bles, clothes with Pa - ris la - bels

Dad - dy! You ought-a get the best for me.

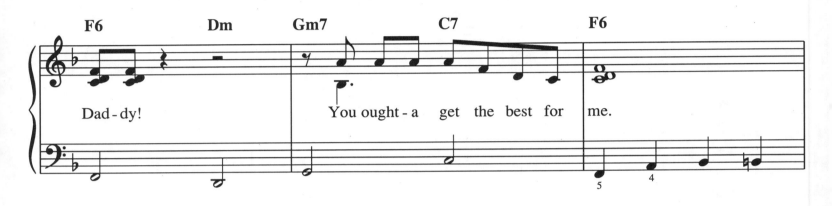

Here's 'na-maz - ing re - vel - a - tion

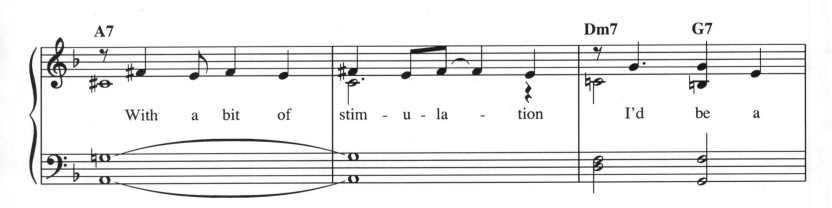

With a bit of stim - u - la - tion I'd be a

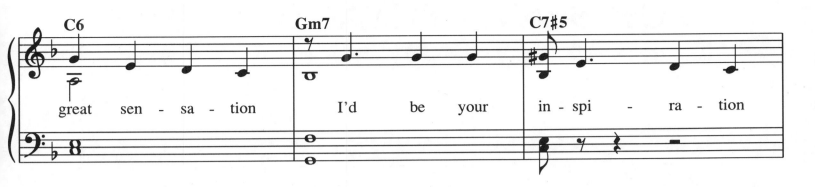

great sen - sa - tion   I'd   be   your   in - spi - ra - tion

Dad-dy!   I want a brand new   car,   cham-pagne,   ca - vi - ar ___

1.

Dad-dy!   You ought-a get the best for   me.   Hey!

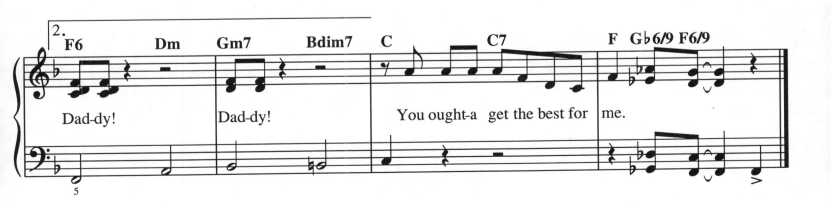

2.

Dad-dy!   Dad-dy!   You ought-a get the best for   me.

5

(I LOVE YOU)
FOR SENTIMENTAL REASONS

Words by DEEK WATSON
Music by WILLIAM BEST

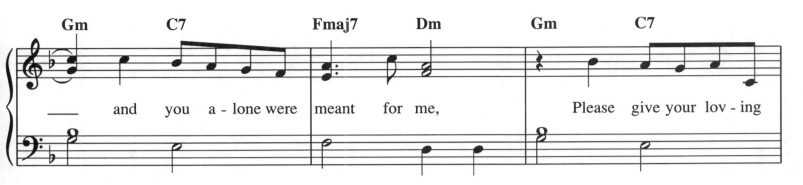

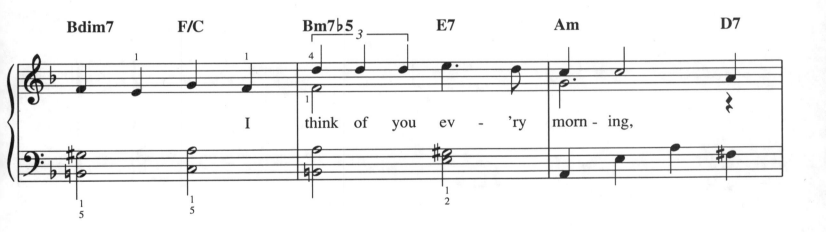

lone - ly when - ev - er you're in sight. I

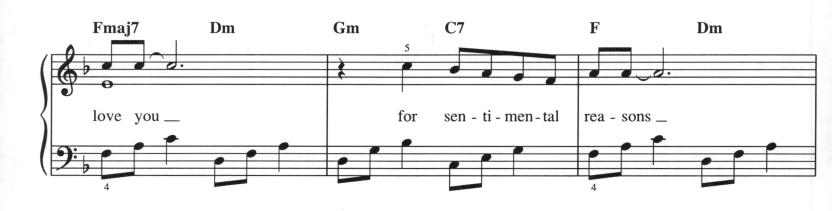

love you __ for sen - ti - men - tal rea - sons __

I have you do be - lieve me, __ I've giv - en you my

heart. I heart. *rit.*

GOD BLESS' THE CHILD

Words and Music by ARTHUR HERZOG JR.
and BILLIE HOLIDAY

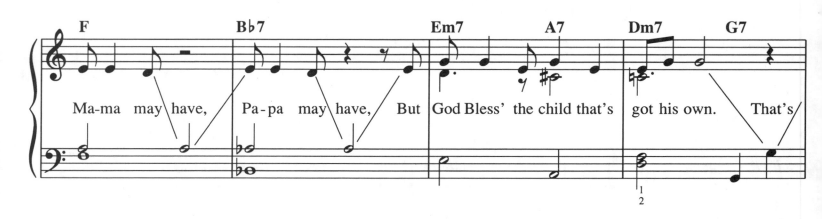

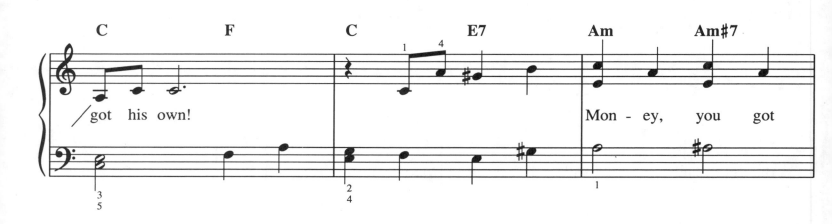

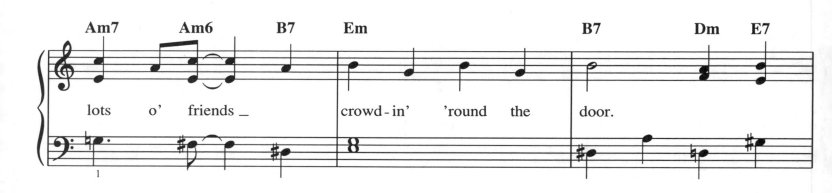

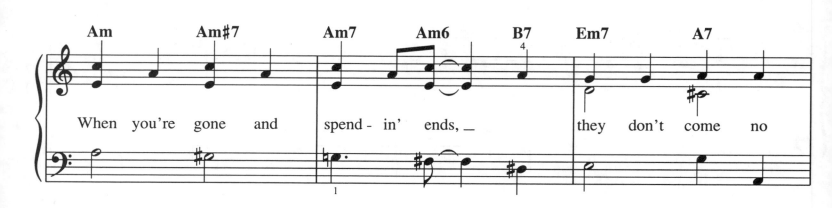

HARLEM NOCTURNE

Words by DICK ROGERS
Music by EARLE HAGEN

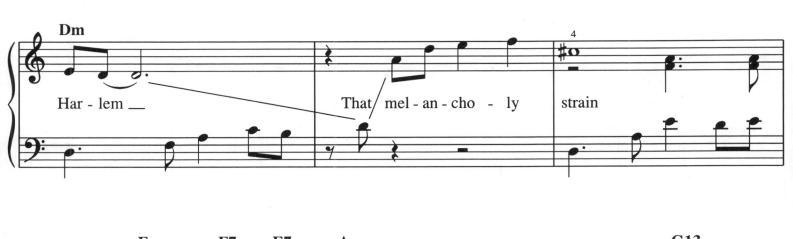

Har - lem — That / mel - an - cho - ly strain

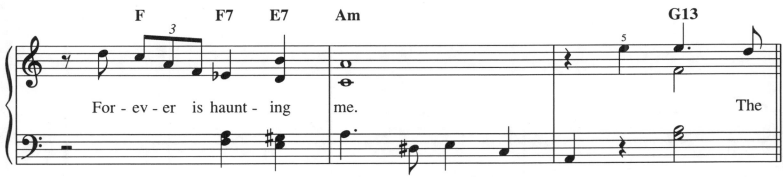

For - ev - er is haunt - ing me. The

(♪♪ played as ♪♪³)

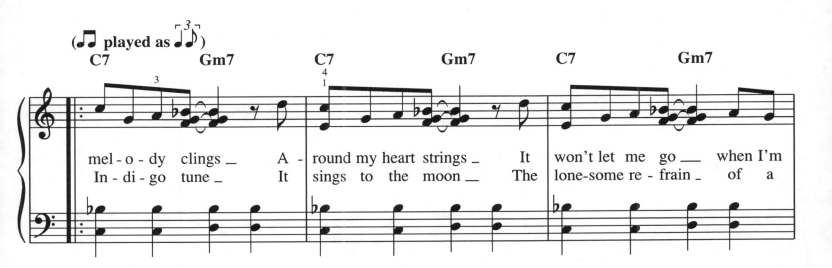

mel - o - dy clings — A - round my heart strings — It won't let me go — when I'm
In - di - go tune — It sings to the moon — The lone-some re - frain — of a

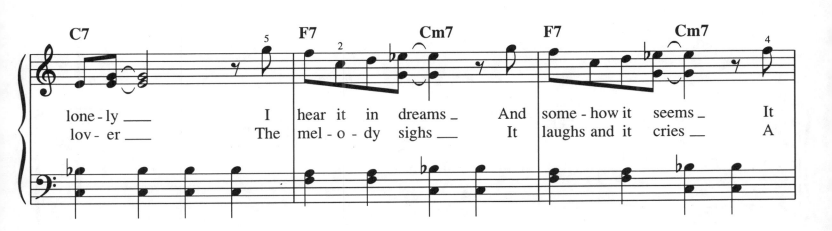

lone - ly — I hear it in dreams — And some - how it seems — It
lov - er — The mel - o - dy sighs — It laughs and it cries — A

makes me weep and   I can't sleep.   An
moon in blue that   walks the long night

thru.   Tho' with the dawn   is   gone

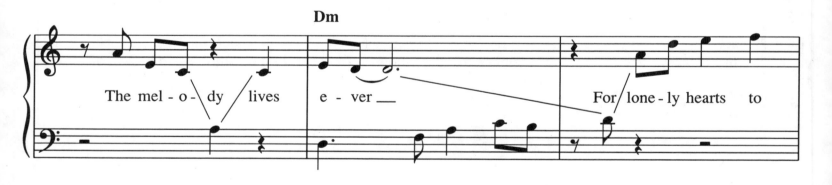

The mel - o - dy   lives   e - ver ___   For lone - ly hearts   to

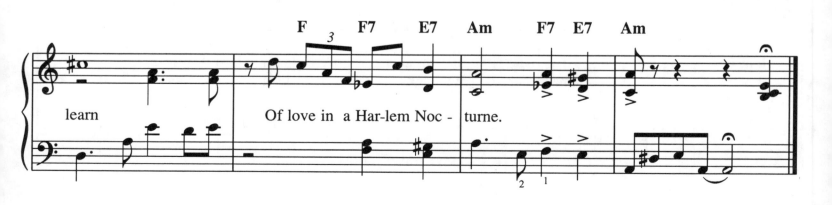

learn   Of love in a Har - lem Noc - turne.

HAVE I TOLD YOU LATELY
THAT I LOVE YOU

Words and Music by SCOTT WISEMAN

MCA music publishing

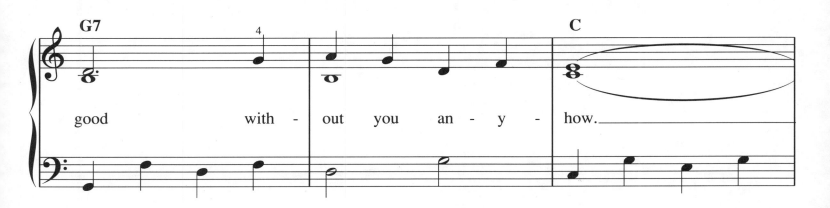

good with - out you an - y - how.

___ Dear, have I told you late - ly that I

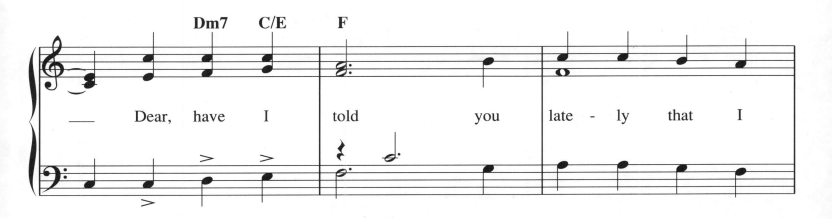

love you? Well, dar - ling, I'm

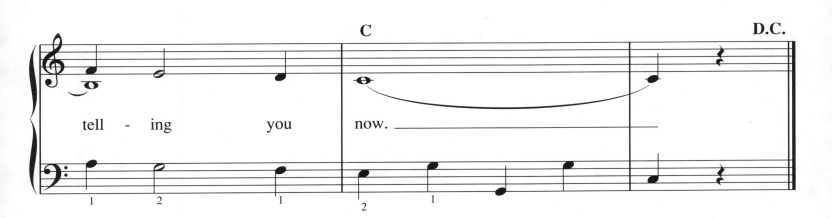

tell - ing you now.

HOW ARE THINGS IN GLOCCA MORRA

(From "FINIAN'S RAINBOW")

Words by E.Y. HARBURG
Music by BURTON LANE

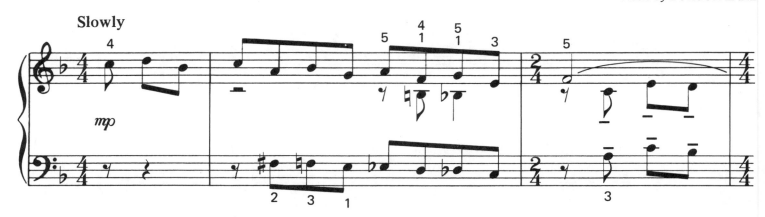

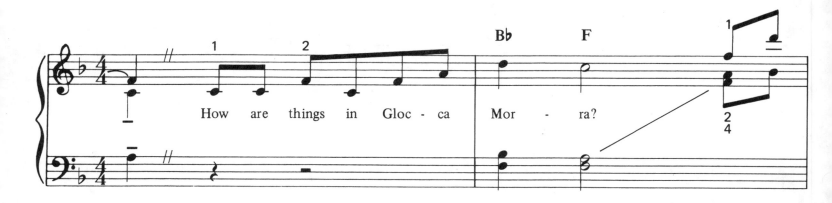

How are things in Gloc - ca Mor - ra?

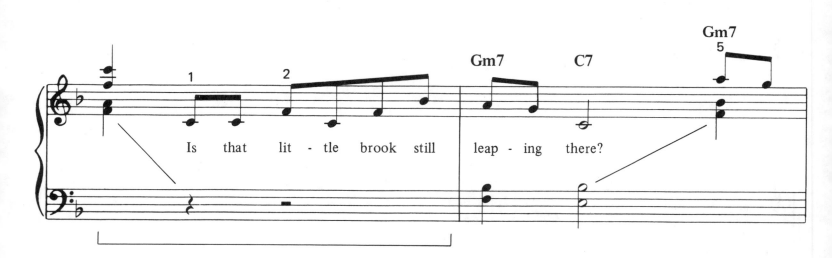

Is that lit - tle brook still leap - ing there?

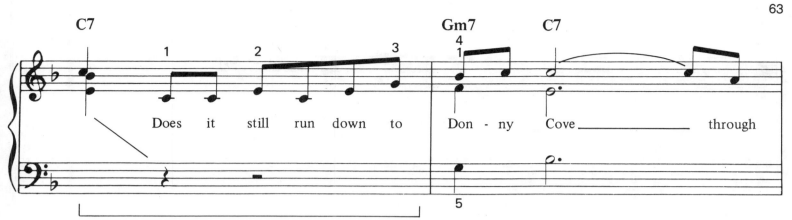

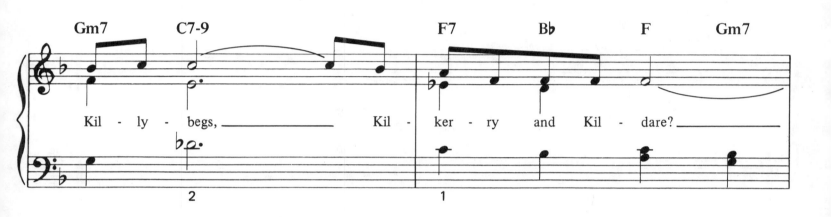

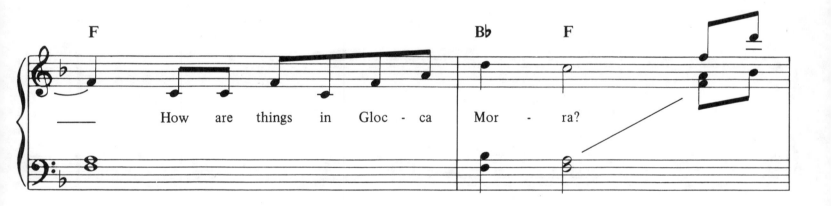

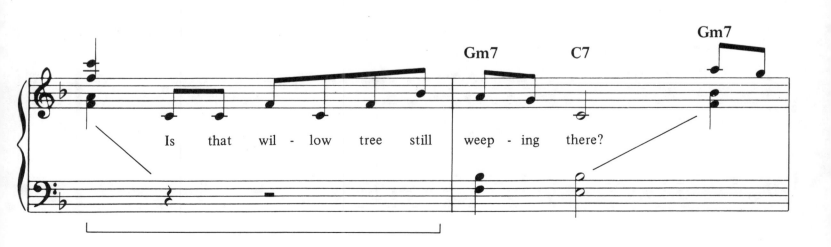

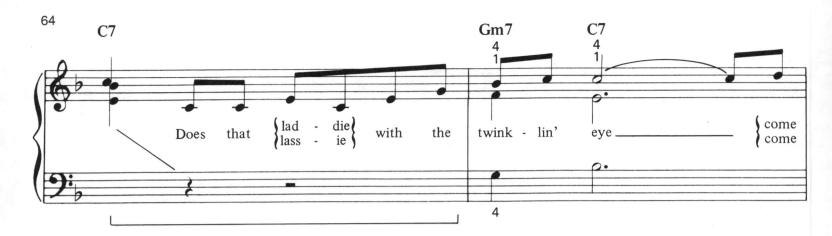

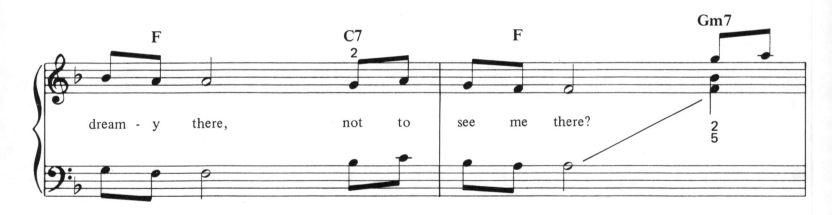

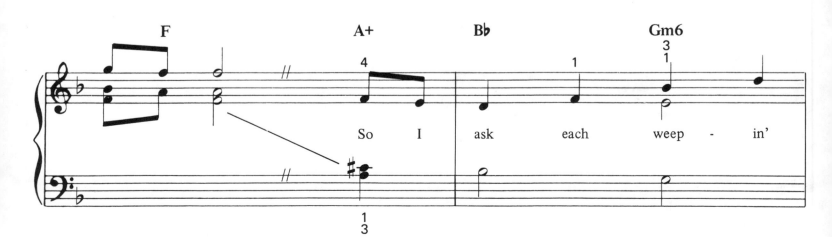

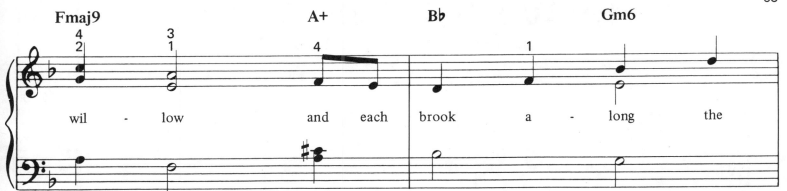

wil - low   and each   brook a - long   the

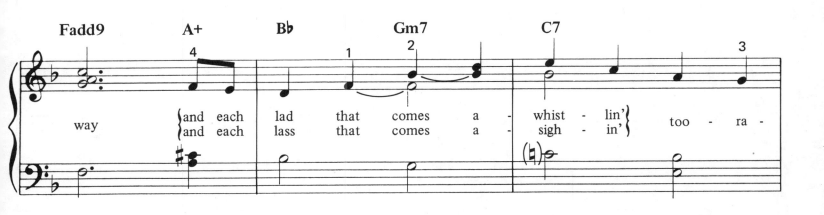

way   {and each   lad   that   comes   a - whist - lin'}   too - ra -
       {and each   lass   that   comes   a - sigh - in'}

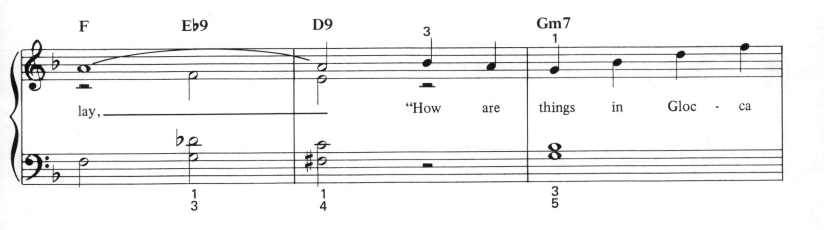

lay, _____   "How   are   things   in   Gloc - ca

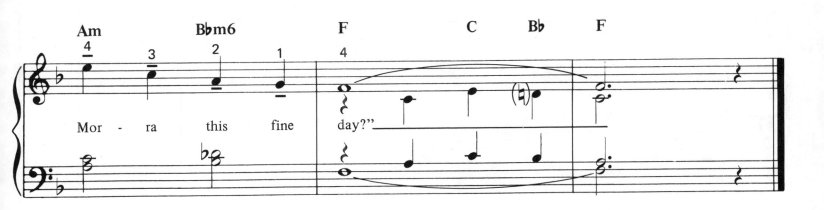

Mor - ra   this   fine   day?" _____

HOW HIGH THE MOON
(From "TWO FOR THE SHOW")

Words by NANCY HAMILTON
Music by MORGAN LEWIS

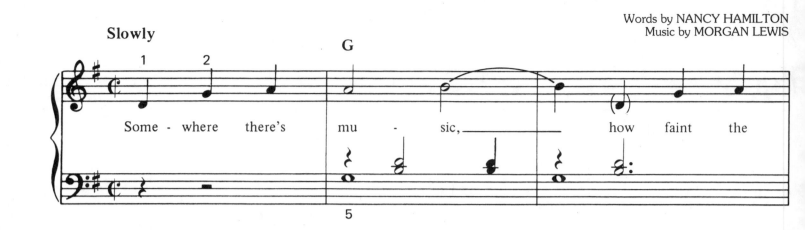

Some - where there's mu - sic, ____ how faint the

tune! _____ Some - where there's heav - en, ____

____ how high the moon! _____ There is no

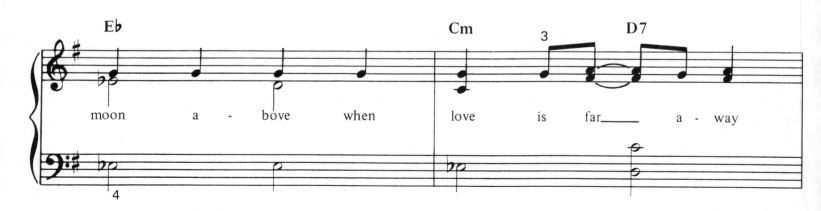

moon a - bove when love is far ____ a - way

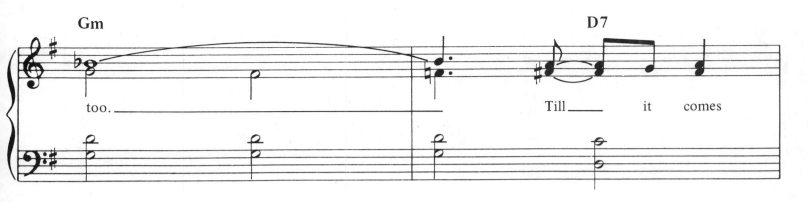

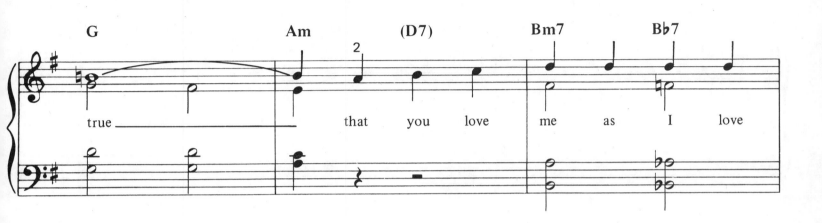

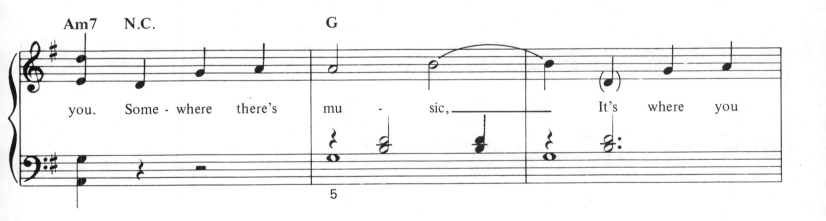

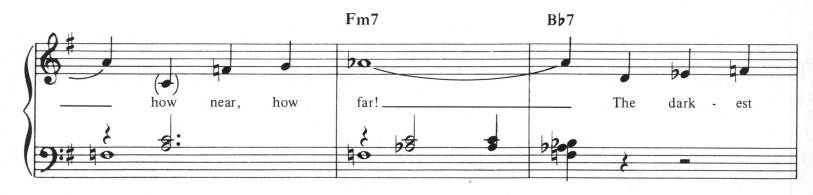

how near, how far! _____ The dark - est

night would shine if you would come___ to me soon.___

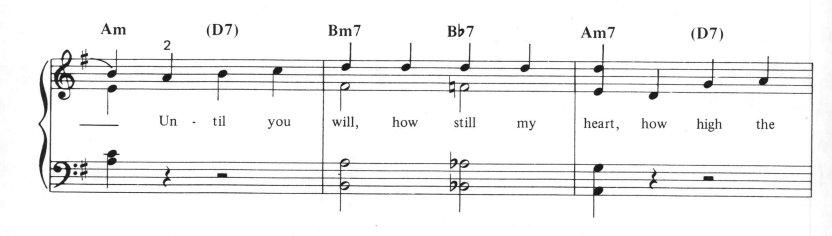

___ Un - til you will, how still my heart, how high the

moon! Some - where there's moon!___

I DON'T WANT TO SET THE WORLD ON FIRE

Words by EDDIE SEILER and SOL MARCUS
Music by BENNIE BENJAMIN and EDDIE DURHAM

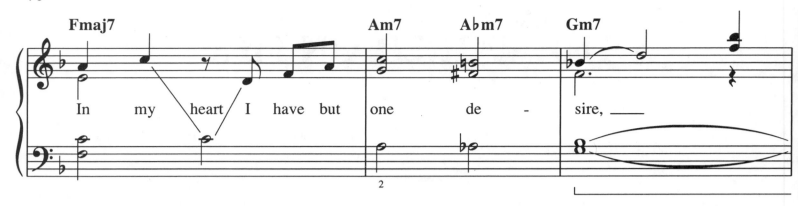

In my heart I have but one de - sire, ___

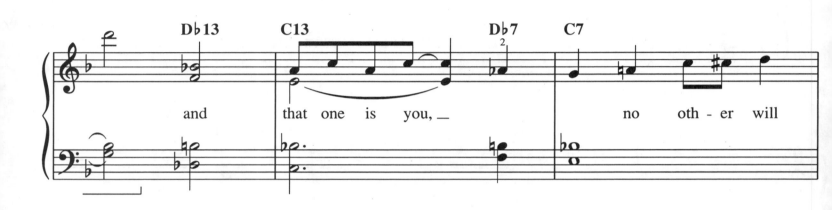

and that one is you, __ no oth - er will

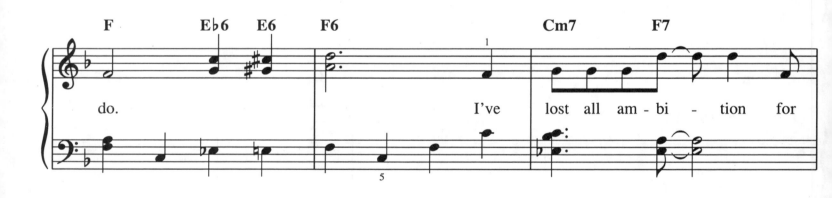

do. I've lost all am - bi - tion for

world-ly ac - claim, __ I just want to be the one you love; and

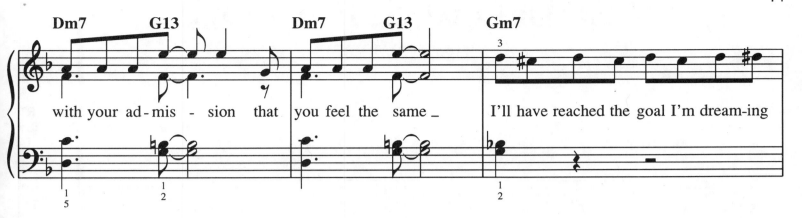

with your ad-mis - sion that you feel the same _ I'll have reached the goal I'm dream-ing

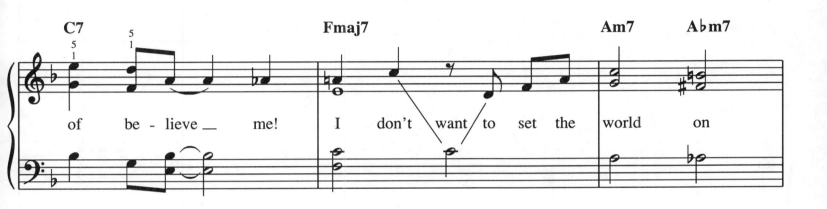

of be - lieve _ me! I don't want to set the world on

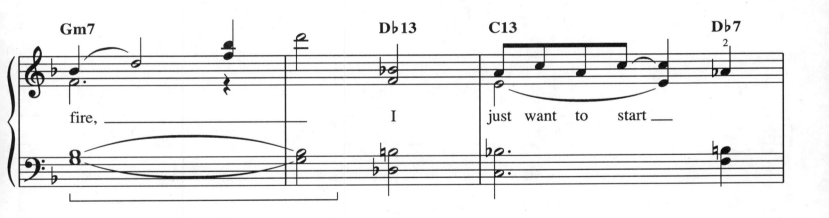

fire, _ I just want to start _

a flame in your heart. *rit.*

I COULD WRITE A BOOK

(From "PAL JOEY")

Words by LORENZ HART
Music by RICHARD RODGERS

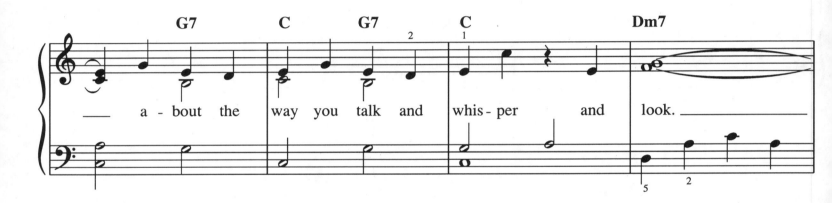

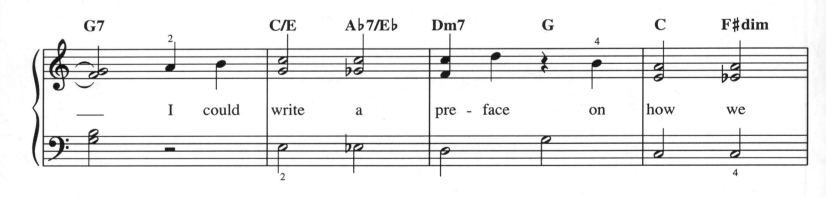

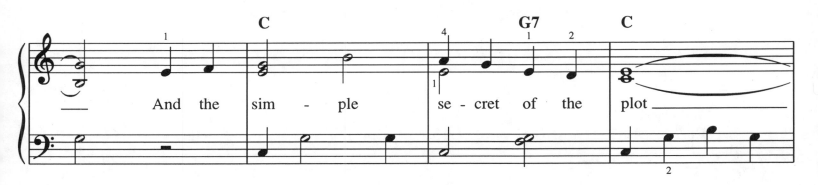

And the sim - ple se - cret of the plot

is just to tell them that I love you a lot.

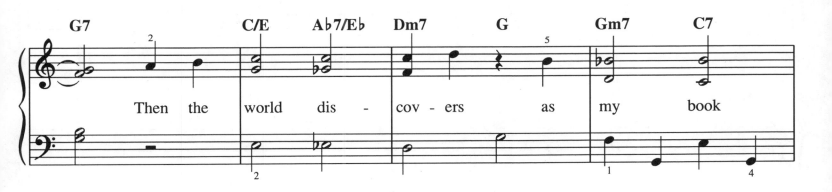

Then the world dis - cov - ers as my book

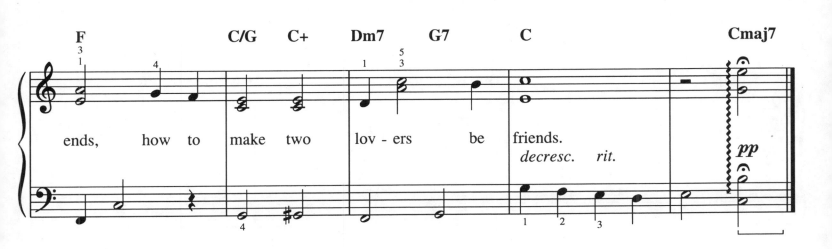

ends, how to make two lov - ers be friends.

decresc. *rit.*

pp

I'LL BE AROUND

Words and Music by
ALEC WILDER

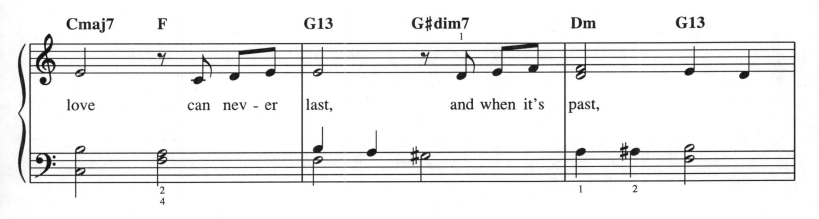

love   can   nev - er   last,   and when it's past,

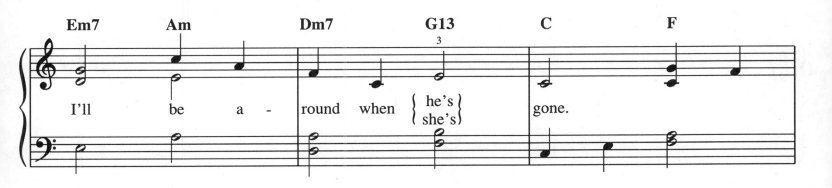

I'll   be   a -   round   when { he's / she's }   gone.

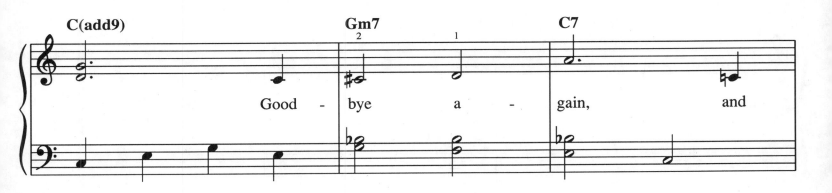

Good - bye   a -   gain,   and

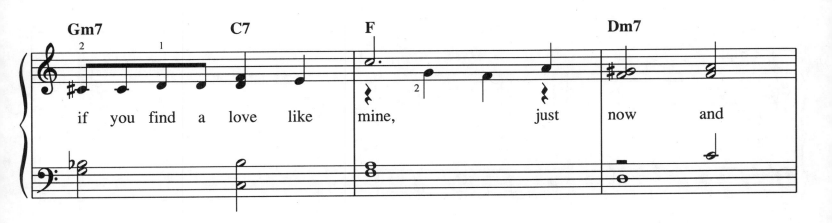

if   you   find   a   love   like   mine,   just   now   and

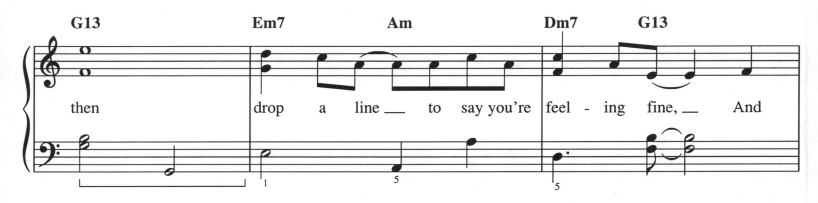

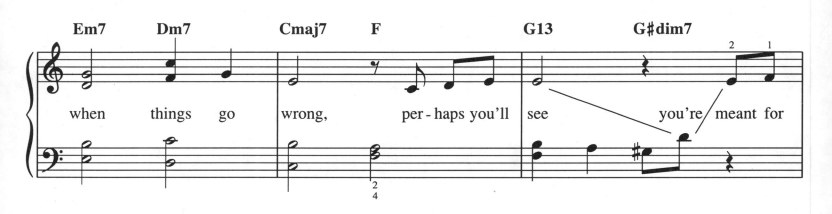

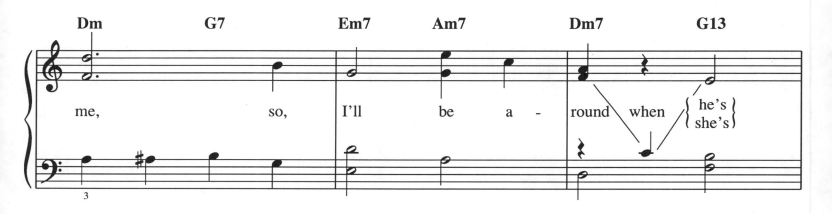

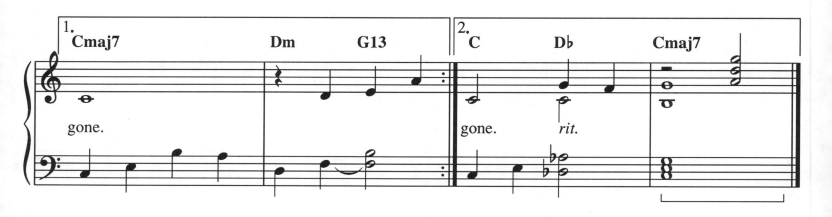

I'M BEGINNING TO SEE THE LIGHT

Words and Music by HARRY JAMES, DUKE ELLINGTON,
JOHNNY HODGES and DON GEORGE

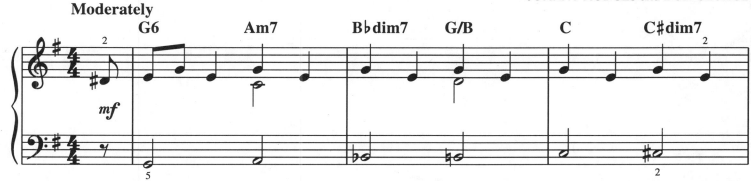

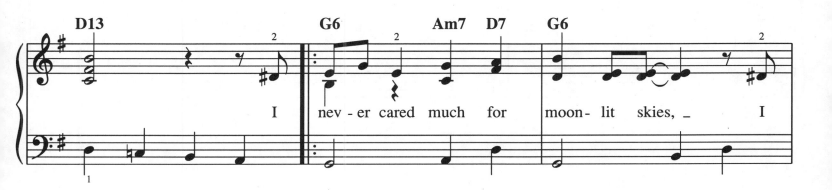

I nev-er cared much for moon-lit skies, __ I

nev-er wink back at fire ___ flies, ___ But now that the stars are

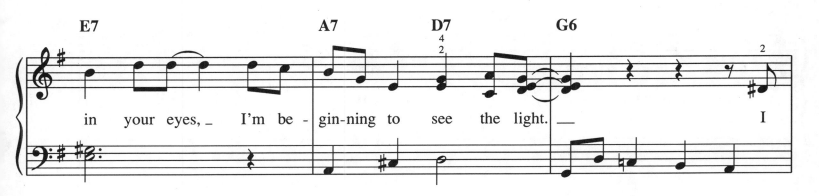

in your eyes, __ I'm be-gin-ning to see the light. __ I

nev - er went in for af - ter glow, _ Or can - dle - light on the

mis - tle - toe, _ But now when you turn the lamp down low _ I'm be -

gin - ning to see the light. _ Used to ram - ble

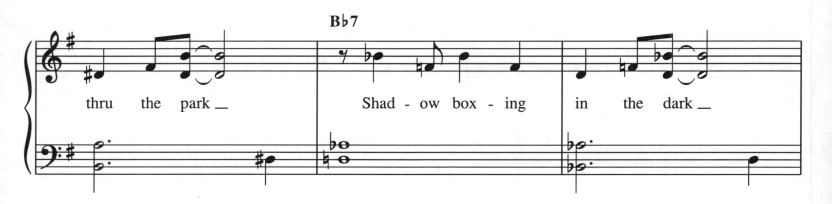

thru the park _ Shad - ow box - ing in the dark _

Then you came and caused a spark, __ That's a four a-larm fire ____

now. I nev-er made love by lan-tern shine, __ I

nev-er saw rain-bows in my wine, __ But now that your lips are

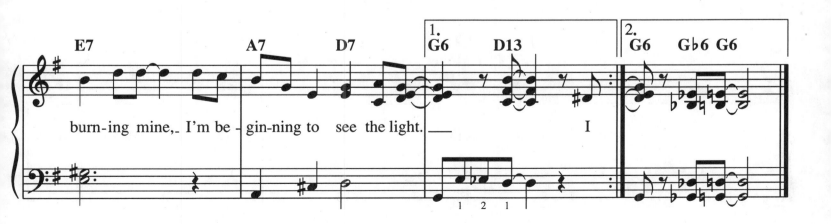

burn-ing mine, __ I'm be-gin-ning to see the light. ____ I

I'LL REMEMBER APRIL

Words and Music by DON RAYE,
GENE DE PAUL and PAT JOHNSON

Moderately fast

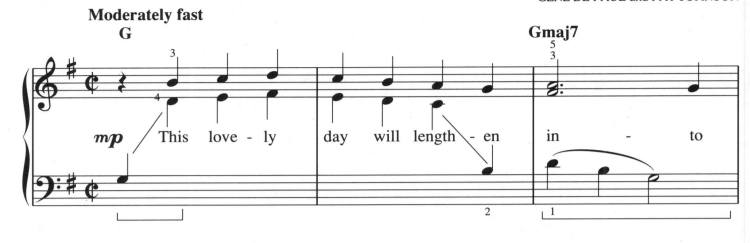

This love-ly day will length-en in - to

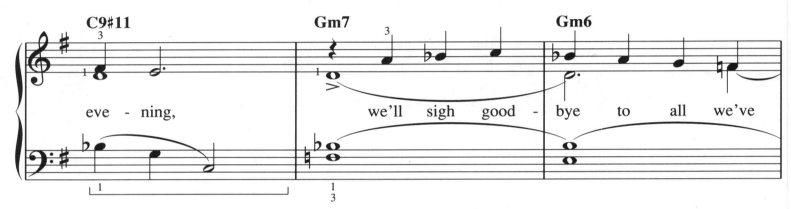

eve - ning, we'll sigh good - bye to all we've

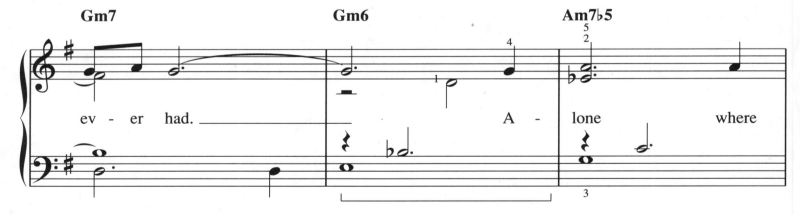

ev - er had. ____ A - lone where

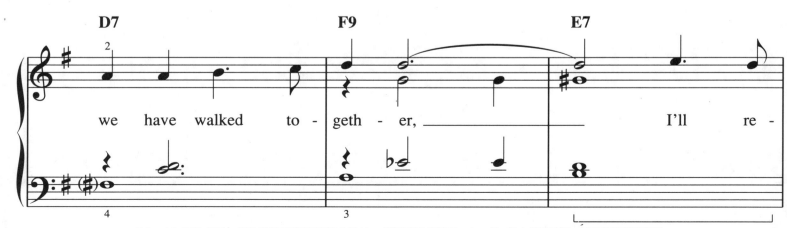

we have walked to-geth-er, ____ I'll re-

MCA music publishing

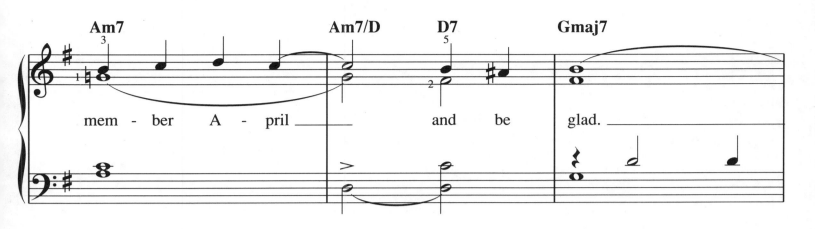

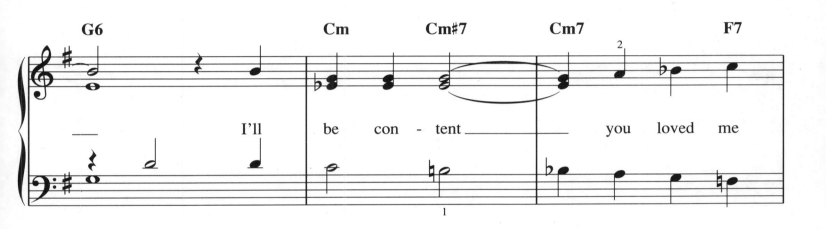

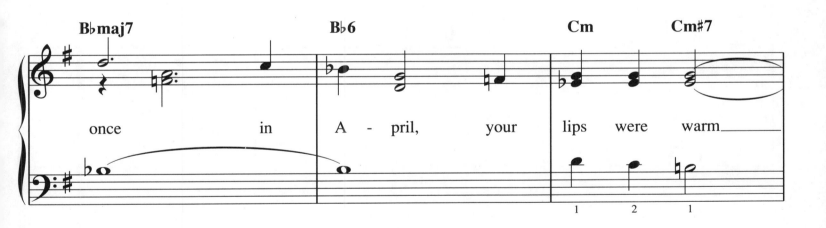

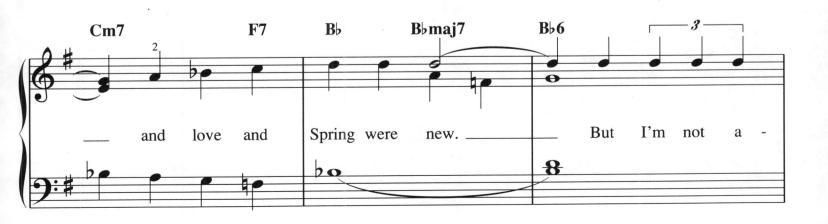

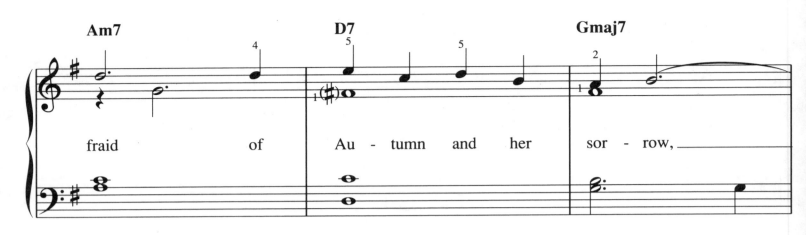

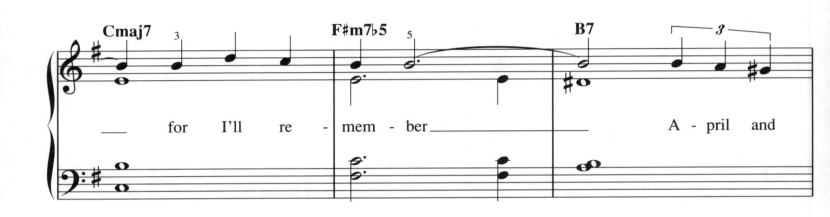

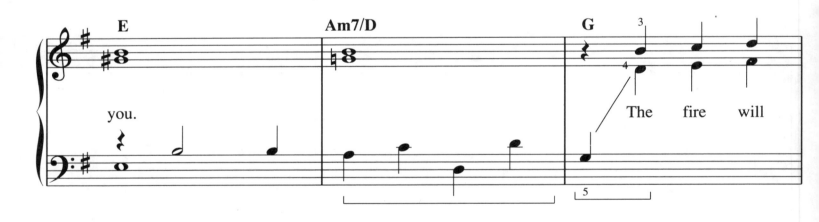

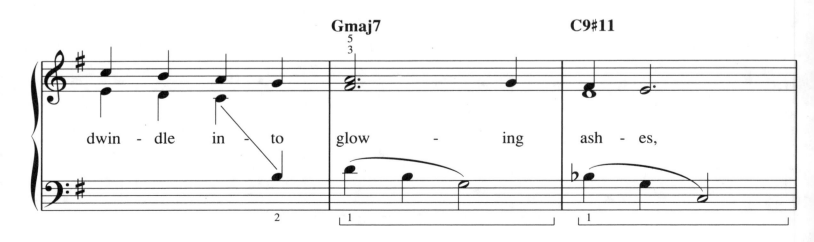

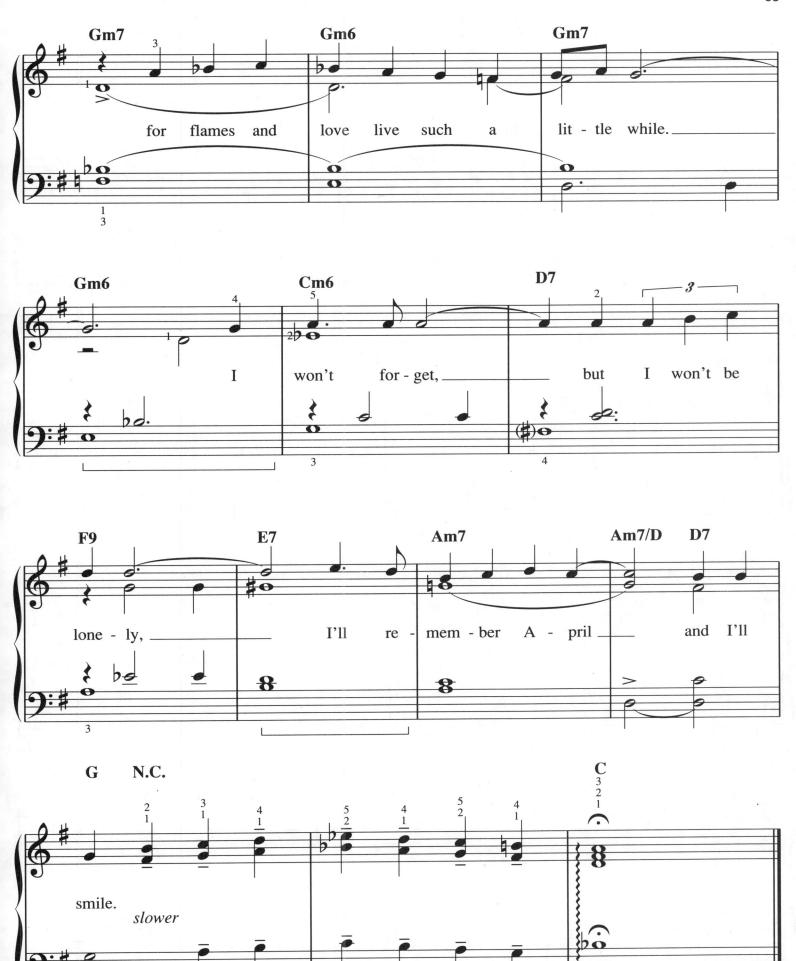

83

IMAGINATION

Words by JOHNNY BURKE
Music by JIMMY VAN HEUSEN

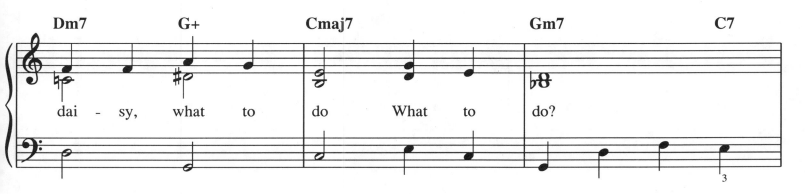

Dm7 · G+ · Cmaj7 · Gm7 · C7

dai - sy, what to do What to do?

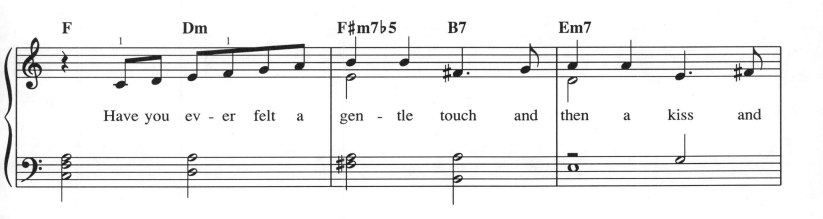

F · Dm · F#m7b5 · B7 · Em7

Have you ev - er felt a gen - tle touch and then a kiss and

Gdim7 · G · Em · Am7 · D7

then and then Find it's on - ly your im - ag - i - na - tion a -

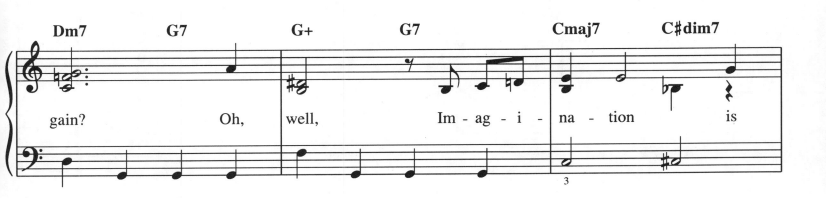

Dm7 · G7 · G+ · G7 · Cmaj7 · C#dim7

gain? Oh, well, Im - ag - i - na - tion is

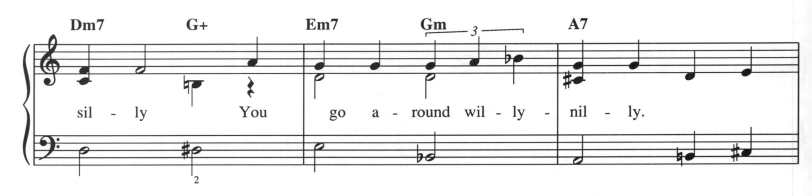

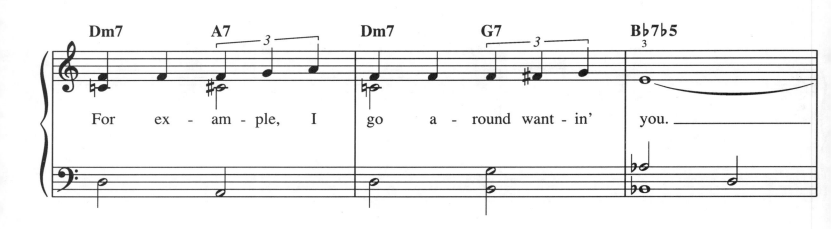

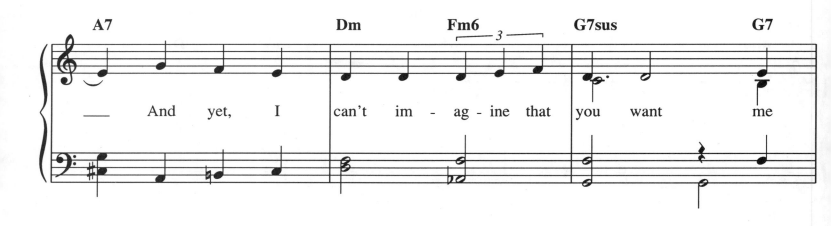

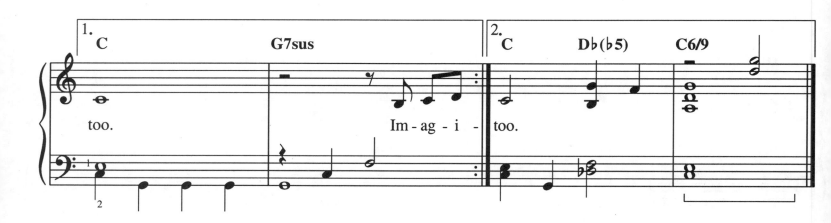

IT'S A GRAND NIGHT FOR SINGING

(From "STATE FAIR")

Lyrics by OSCAR HAMMERSTEIN II
Music by RICHARD RODGERS

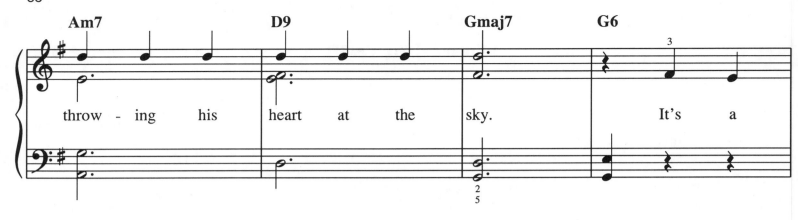

throw - ing his heart at the sky. It's a

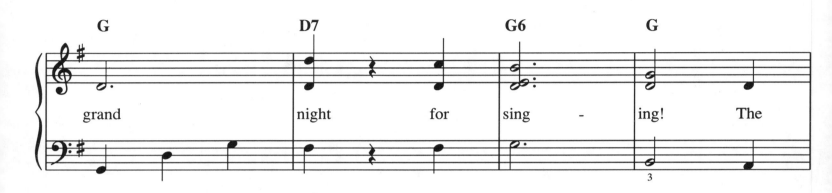

grand night for sing - ing! The

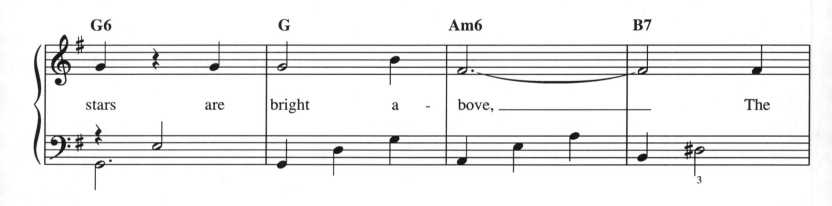

stars are bright a - bove, _____ The

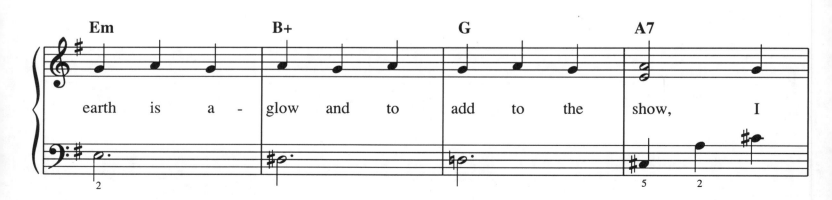

earth is a - glow and to add to the show, I

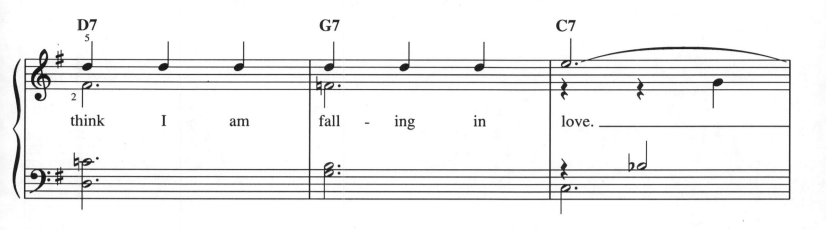

think   I   am   fall - ing   in   love. _____

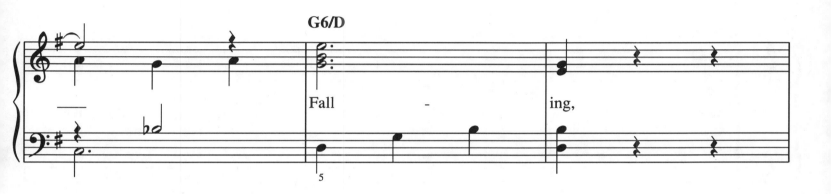

_____   Fall   -   ing,

fall   -   ing   in   love

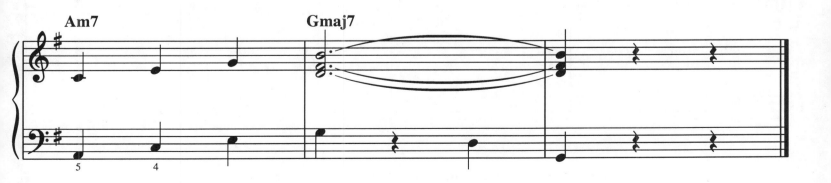

IT'S A MOST UNUSUAL DAY

Words by HAROLD ADAMSON
Music by JIMMY McHUGH

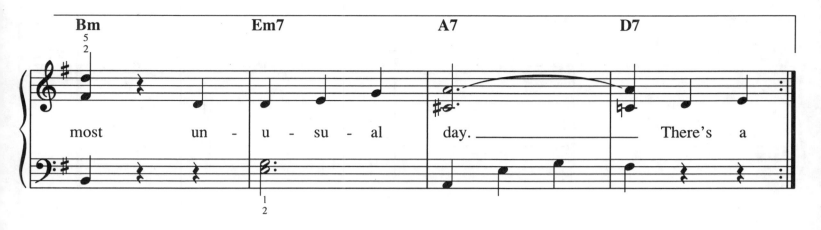

most un - u - su - al day. _____ There's a

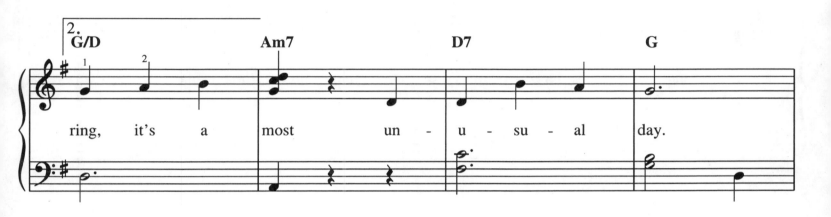

ring, it's a most un - u - su - al day.

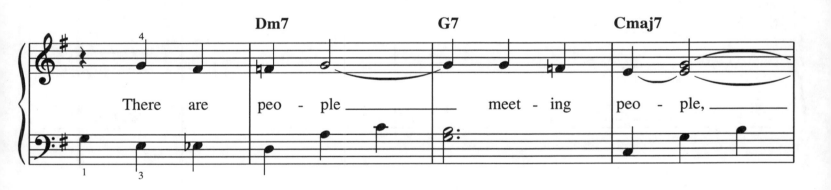

There are peo - ple _____ meet - ing peo - ple, _____

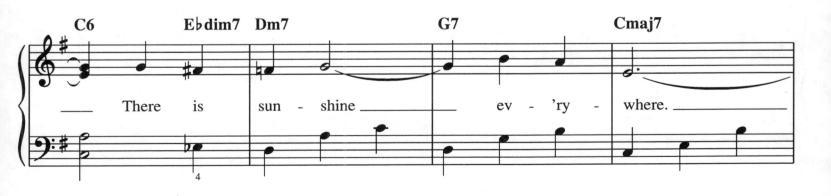

_____ There is sun - shine _____ ev - 'ry - where. _____

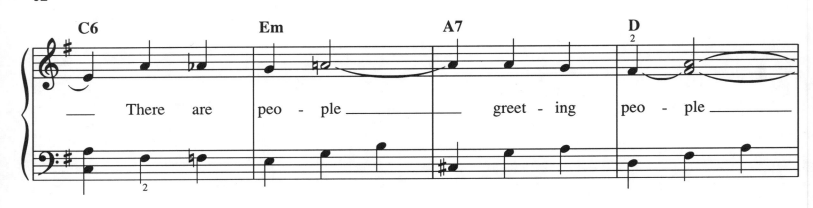

There are peo - ple _____ greet - ing peo - ple _____

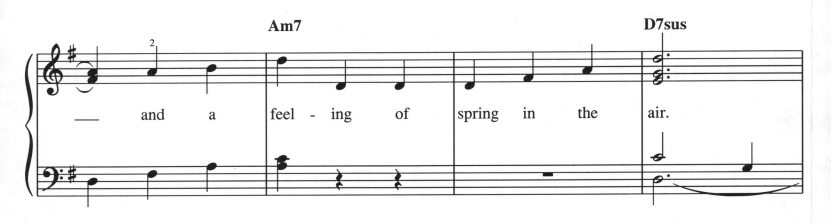

_____ and a feel - ing of spring in the air.

It's a most un - u - su - al time, _____

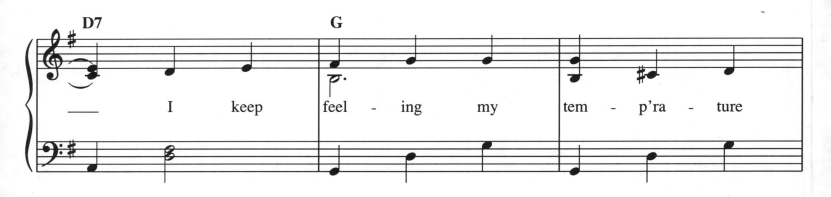

_____ I keep feel - ing my tem - p'ra - ture

climb. If my heart won't be - have in the

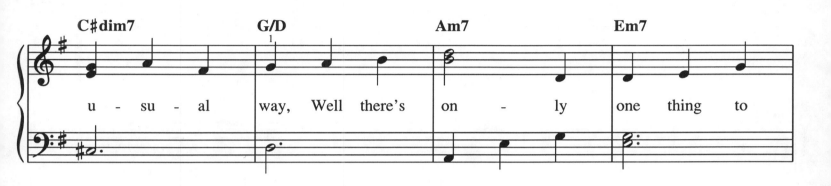

u - su - al way, Well there's on - ly one thing to

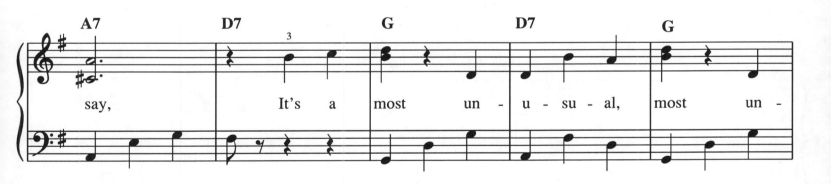

say, It's a most un - u - su - al, most un -

u - su - al, most un - u - su - al day.

JUKE BOX SATURDAY NIGHT

Words by AL STILLMAN
Music by PAUL McGRANE

F

Good-man and Ky - ser and Mil - ler ___ Help to make things

F7   **Bb**

bright, Mix-in' hot licks with va - nil - la, ___

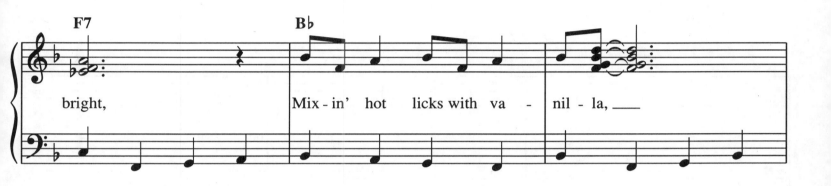

Am   **Abdim7 Gm7**   **C7**   **F**   **Cm7**   **F7**

Juke Box Sat - ur - day Night. They put noth - in'

Cm7   **F7**   **Bb**   **F+**   **Bb**

past us, ___ Me and hon - ey lamb, ___

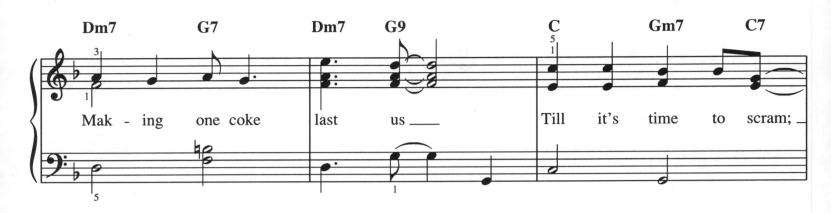

Mak - ing one coke last us ___ Till it's time to scram; ___

___ Mon - ey, we real - ly don't need that, ___

We make out all right, Let - tin' the oth - er guy

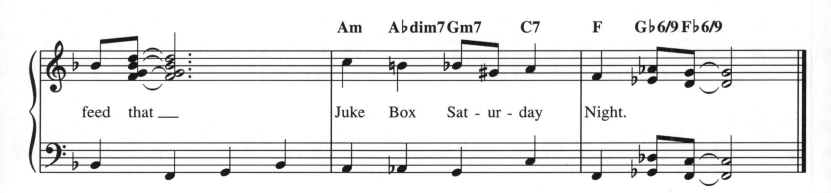

feed that ___ Juke Box Sat - ur - day Night.

JUNE IS BUSTIN' OUT ALL OVER

(From "CAROUSEL")

Lyrics by OSCAR HAMMERSTEIN II
Music by RICHARD RODGERS

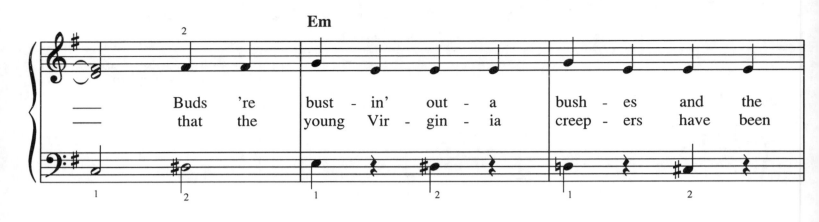

Buds 're / that the bust-in' out a / young Vir - gin - ia bush - es and the / creep - ers have been

Em

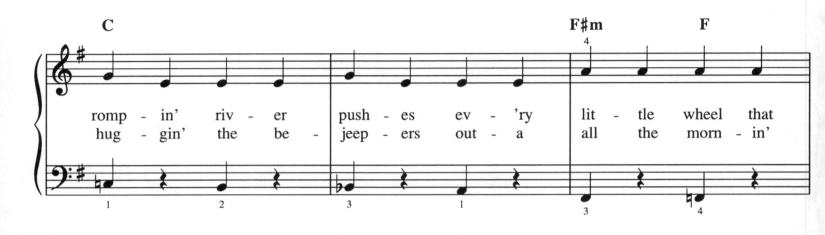

romp - in' riv - er / hug - gin' the be - push - es ev - 'ry / jeep - ers out a lit - tle wheel that / all the morn - in'

C   **F♯m**   **F**

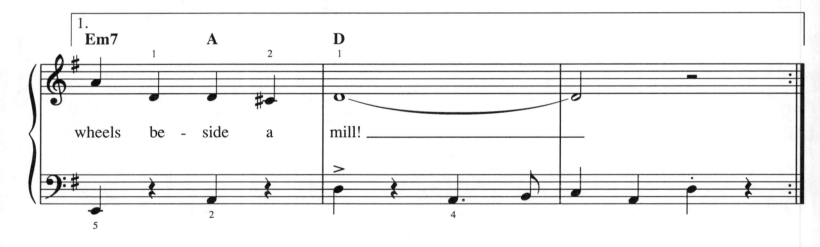

1.
Em7   **A**   **D**

wheels be - side a mill! ___

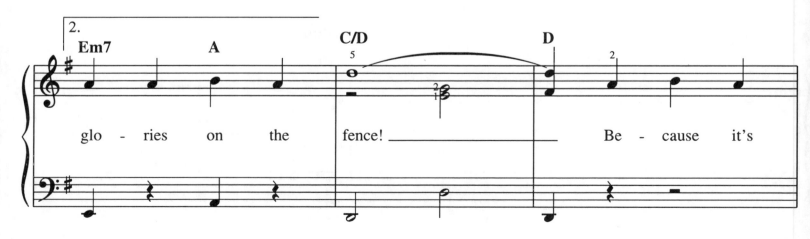

2.
Em7   **A**   **C/D**   **D**

glo - ries on the fence! ___ Be - cause it's

THE LAST TIME I SAW PARIS

Words by OSCAR HAMMERSTEIN II
Music by JEROME KERN

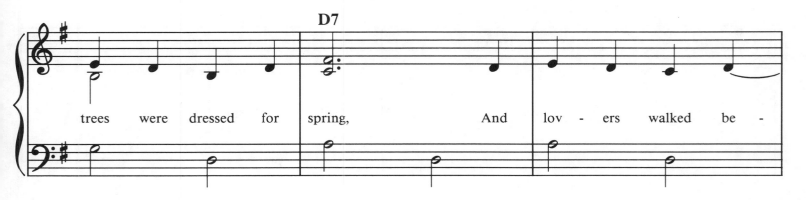

trees were dressed for spring, And lov - ers walked be -

neath those trees, And birds found songs to sing. I

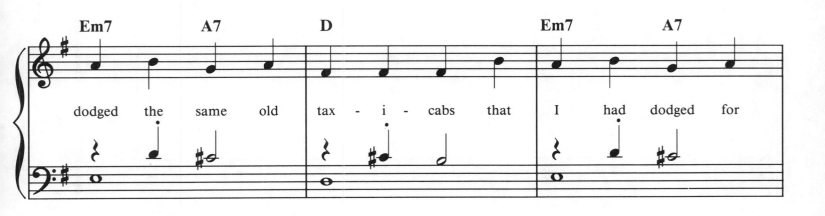

dodged the same old tax - i - cabs that I had dodged for

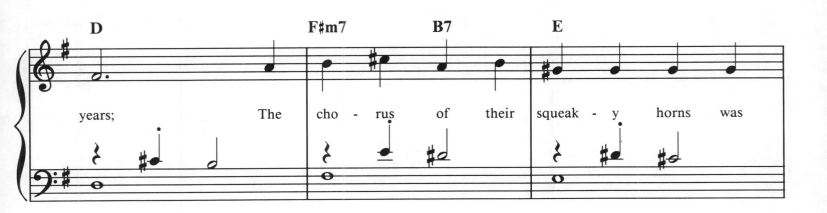

years; The cho - rus of their squeak - y horns was

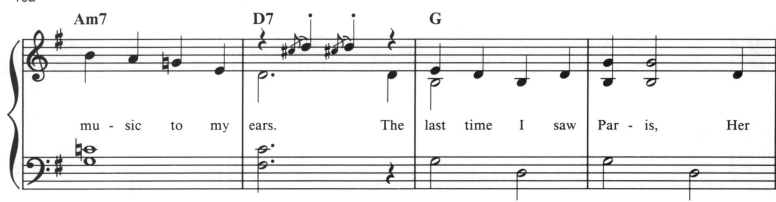

mu - sic to my ears. The last time I saw Par - is, Her

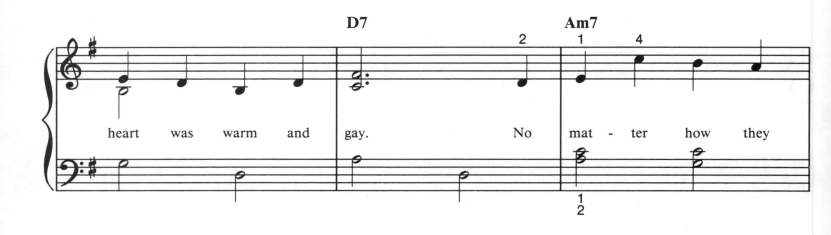

heart was warm and gay. No mat - ter how they

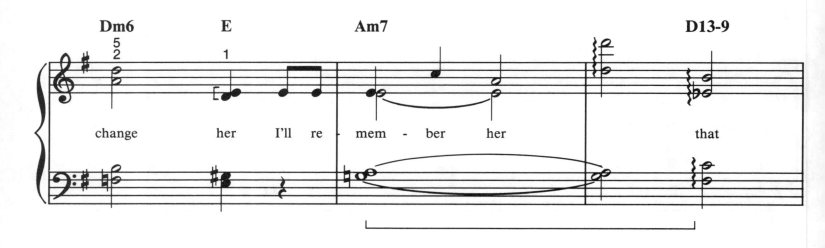

change her I'll re - mem - ber her that

way. The way.

LILLI MARLENE

German Lyric by HANS LEIP
English Lyric by TOMMIE CONNOR
Music by NORBERT SCHULTZE

MAIRZY DOATS

Words and Music by MILTON DRAKE,
AL HOFFMAN and JERRY LIVINGSTON

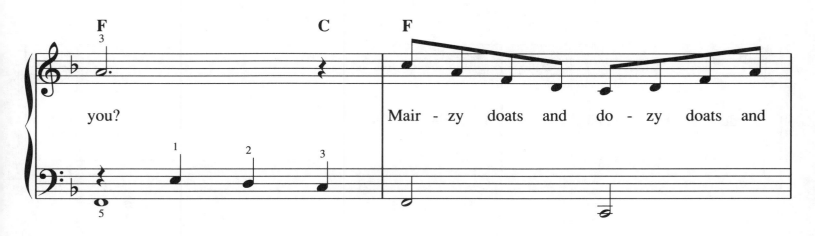

you?

Mair - zy doats and do - zy doats and

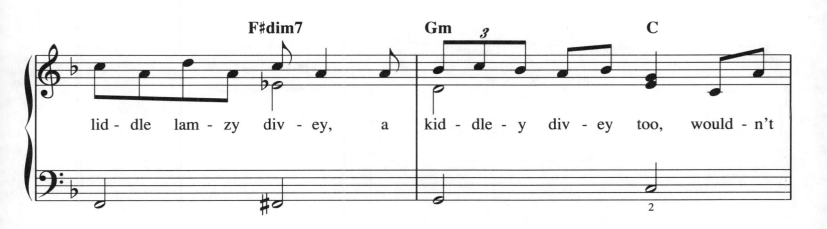

lid - dle lam - zy div - ey, a kid - dle - y div - ey too, would - n't

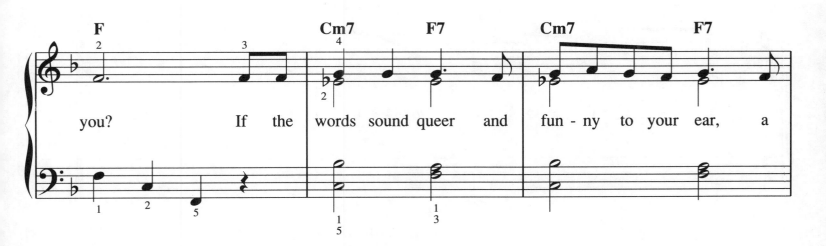

you? If the words sound queer and fun - ny to your ear, a

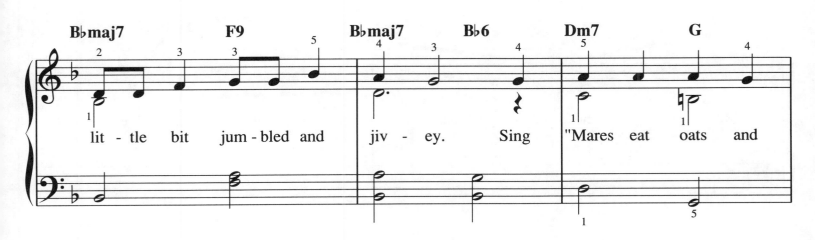

lit - tle bit jum - bled and jiv - ey. Sing "Mares eat oats and

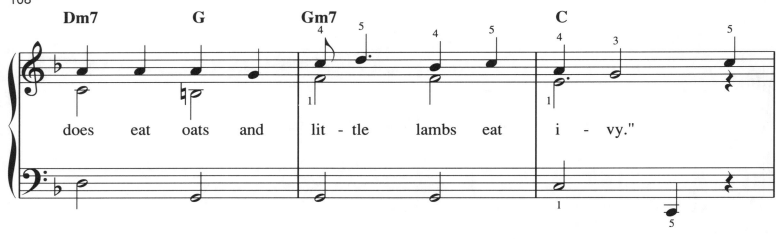

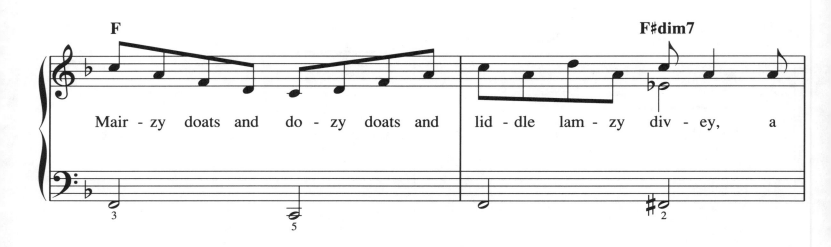

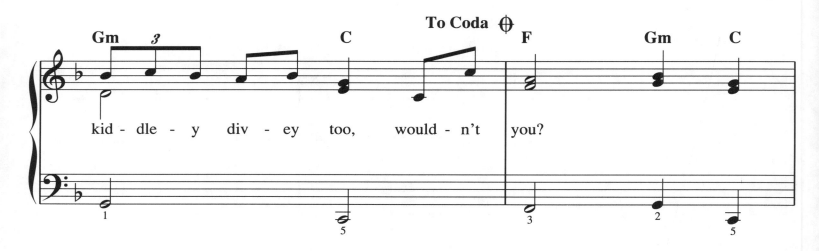

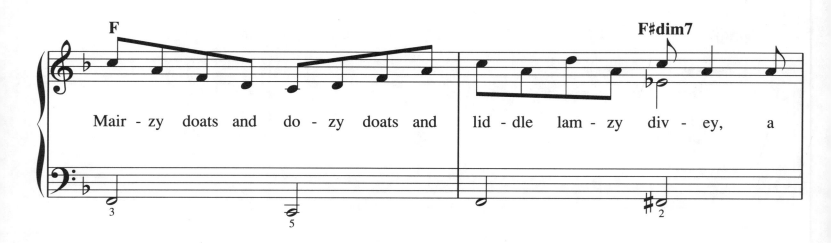

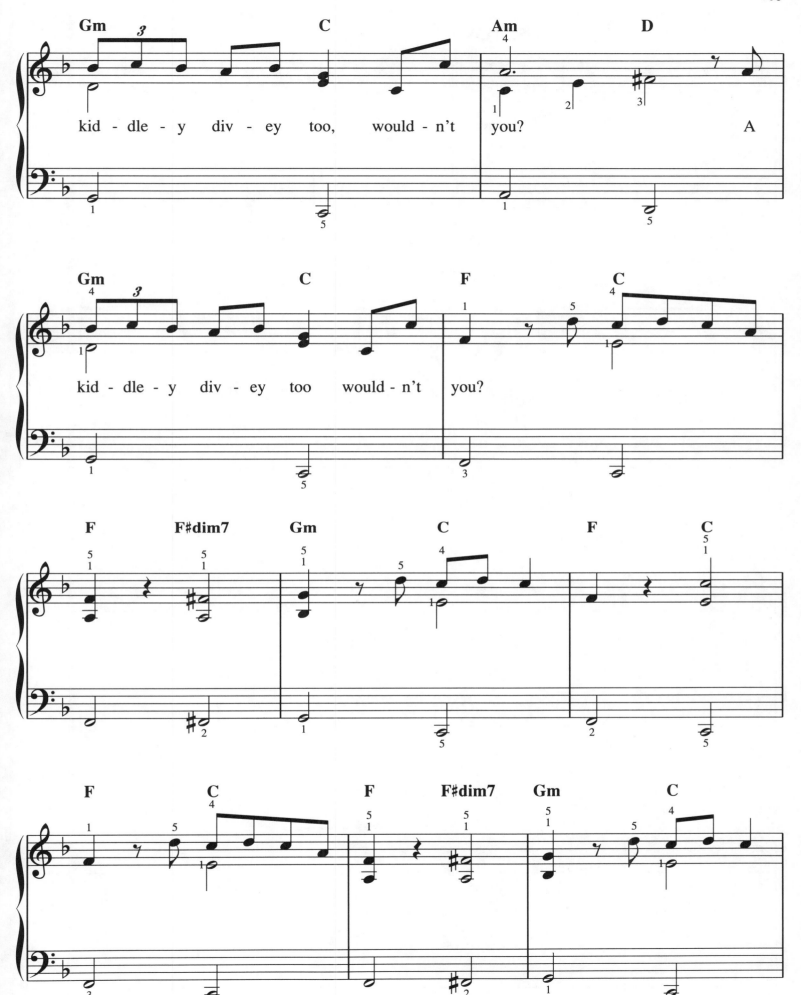

kid - dle - y div - ey too, would - n't you?

A

kid - dle - y div - ey too would - n't you?

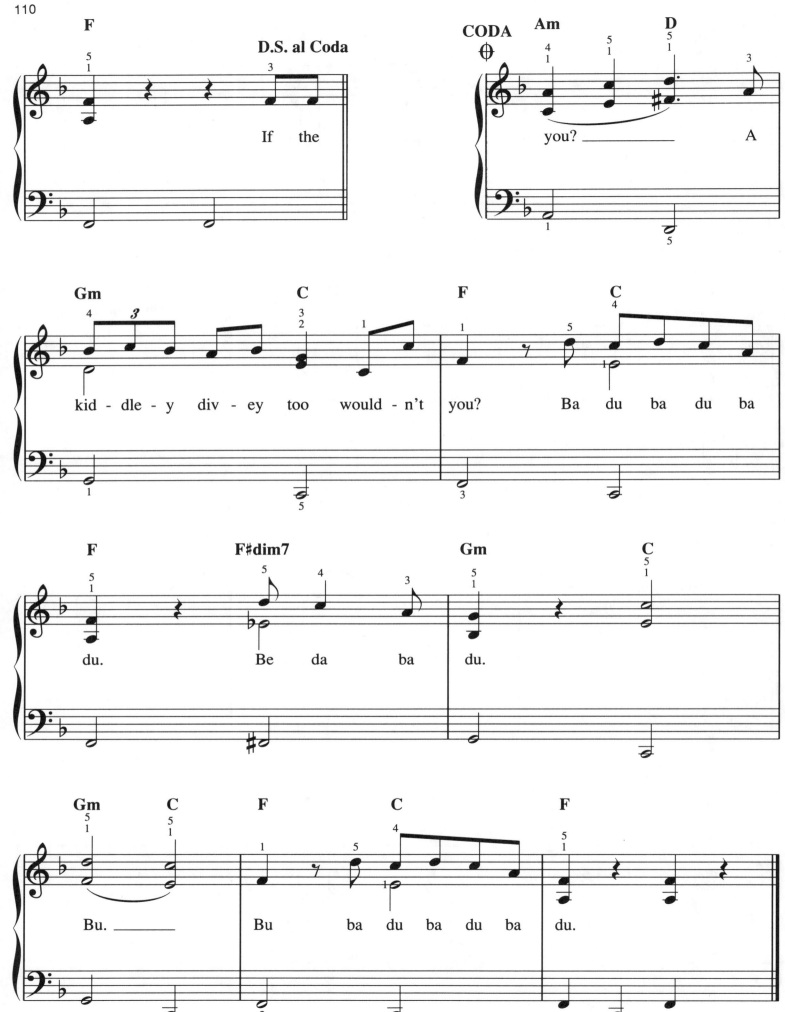

MANAGUA, NICARAGUA

Words by ALBERT GAMSE
Music by IRVING FIELDS

Ma- na- gua, Ni- ca- ra- gua, is a beau-ti-ful town, You

buy a "ha-ci-en-da" for a few "pe-sos" down. You give it to the la-dy you are

try- in' to win But her pa-pa does-n't let you come in. Ma-

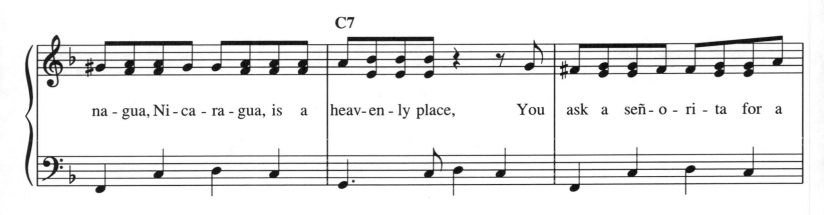

na - gua, Ni - ca - ra - gua, is a heav-en - ly place, You ask a señ - o - ri - ta for a

"leet - tle" em - brace, She an - swers you: "Ca - ram - ba! Scram - ba, Bam - ba - ri - to."

In Ma - na - gua, Ni - ca - ra - gua, that's "No." I have been to man - y trop - ic

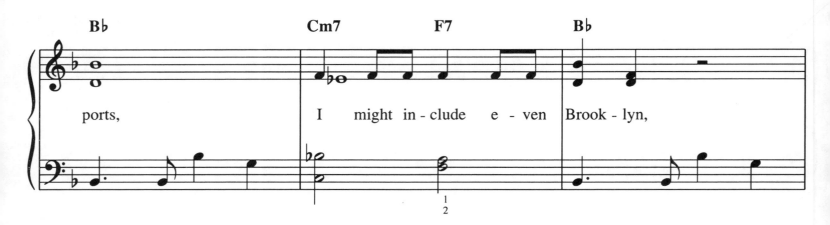

ports, I might in - clude e - ven Brook - lyn,

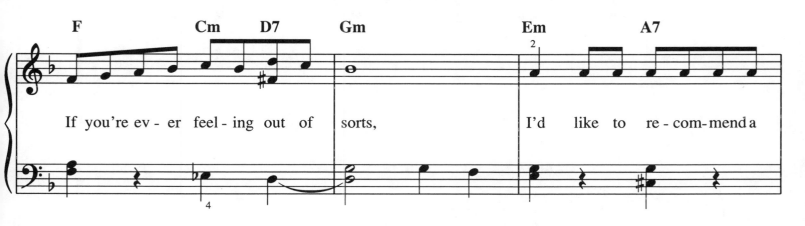

If you're ev - er feel - ing out of sorts, I'd like to re - com - mend a

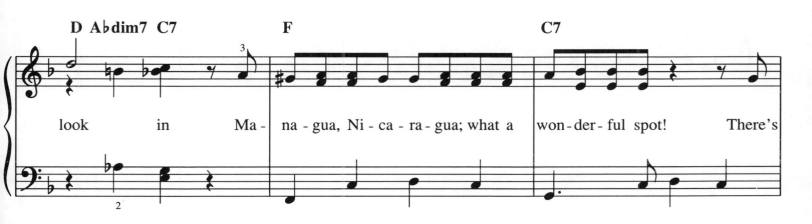

look in Ma - na - gua, Ni - ca - ra - gua; what a won - der - ful spot! There's

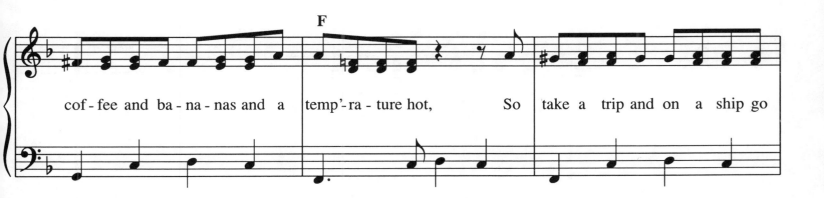

cof - fee and ba - na - nas and a temp'- ra - ture hot, So take a trip and on a ship go

sail - ing a - way, A - cross the "a - gua" to Ma - na - gua, Ni - ca - ra - gua, O - le!

MOONLIGHT IN VERMONT

Words and Music by JOHN BLACKBURN
and KARL SUESSDORF

Freely

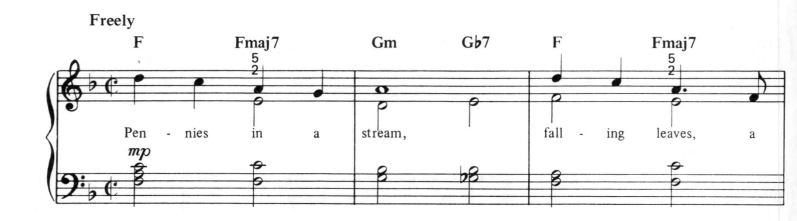

Pen - nies in a stream, fall - ing leaves, a

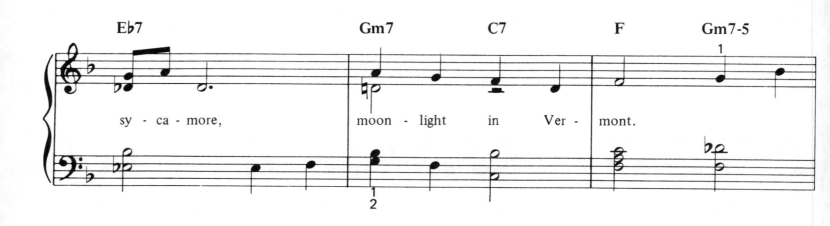

sy - ca - more, moon - light in Ver - mont.

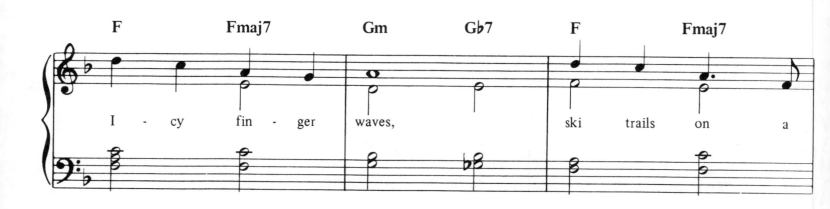

I - cy fin - ger waves, ski trails on a

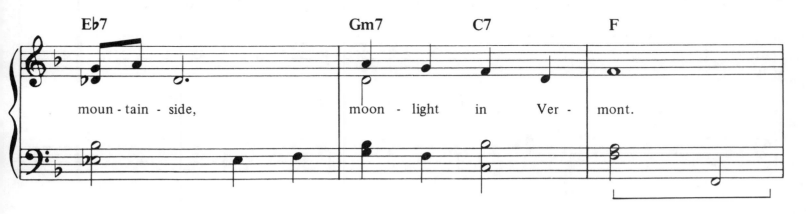

moun - tain - side, moon - light in Ver - mont.

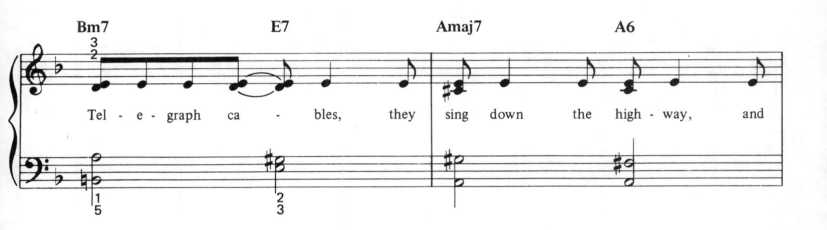

Tel - e - graph ca - bles, they sing down the high - way, and

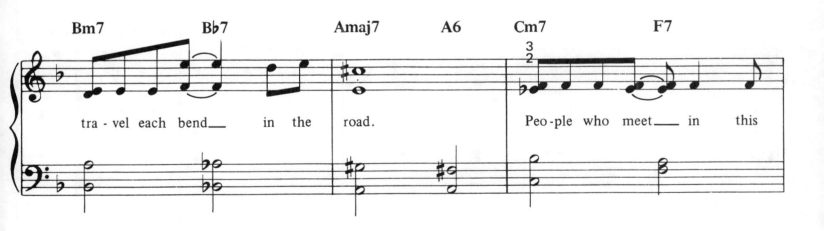

tra - vel each bend___ in the road. Peo - ple who meet___ in this

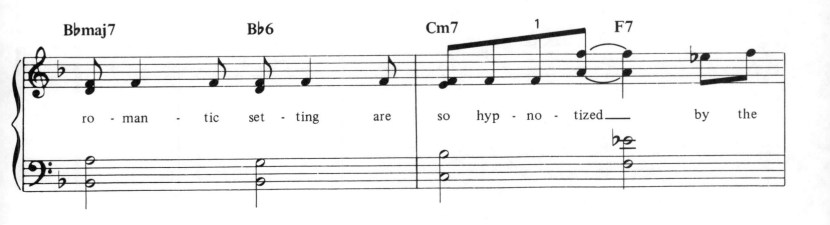

ro - man - tic set - ting are so hyp - no - tized___ by the

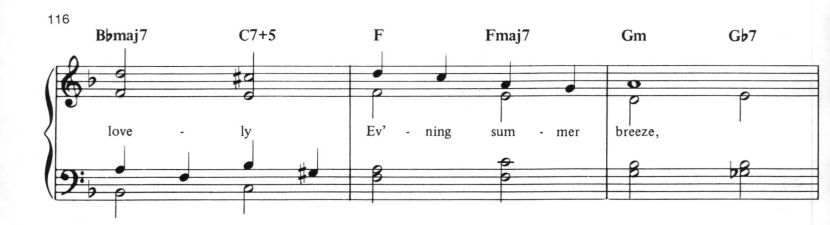

love - ly   Ev' - ning sum - mer breeze,

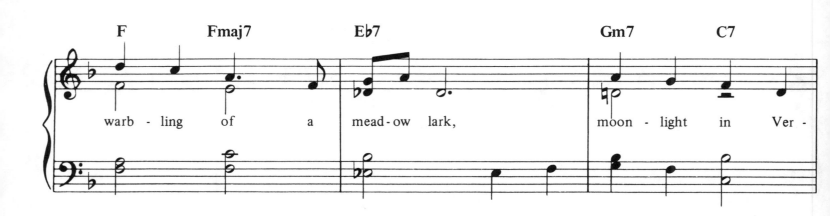

warb - ling of   a   mead-ow lark,   moon - light in Ver -

mont,   You and I and moon - light in Ver -

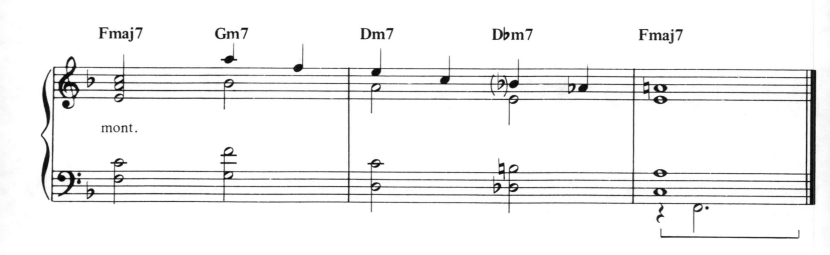

mont.

OKLAHOMA
(From "OKLAHOMA!")

Lyrics by OSCAR HAMMERSTEIN II
Music by RICHARD RODGERS

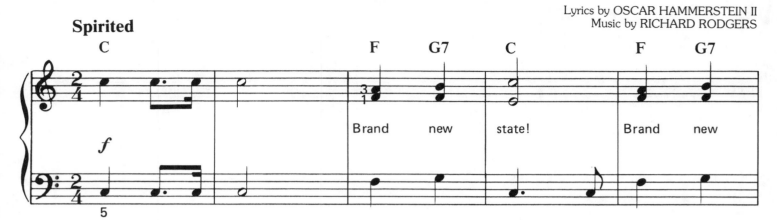

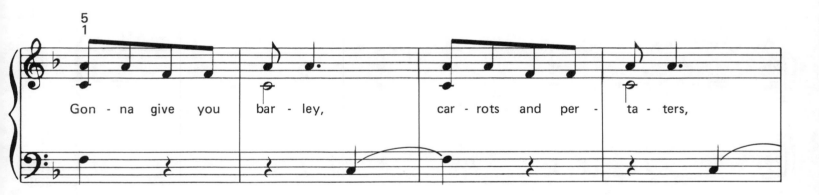

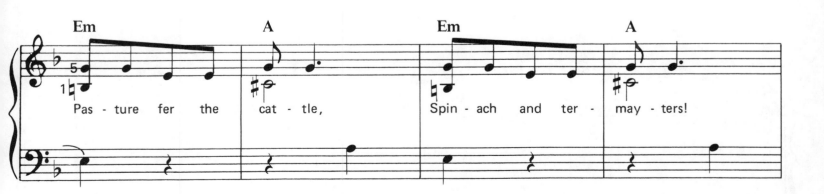

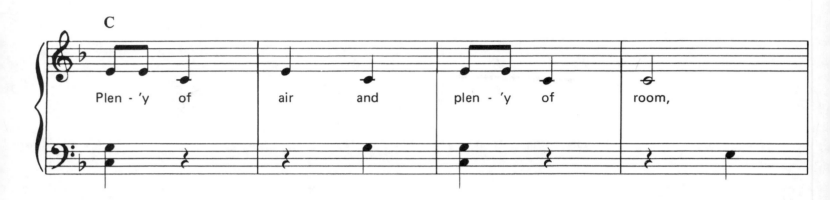

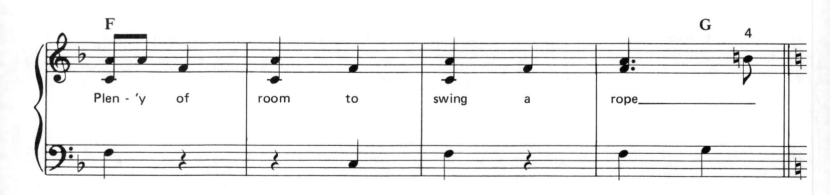

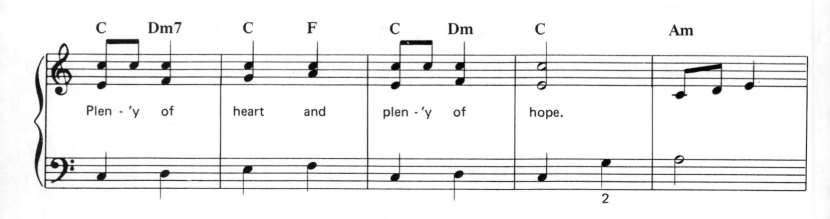

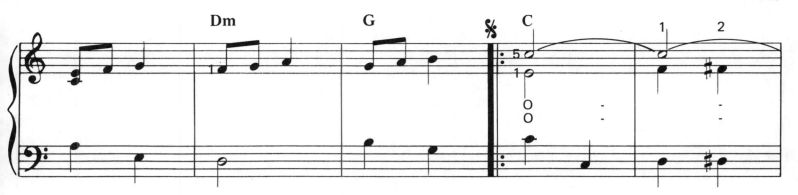

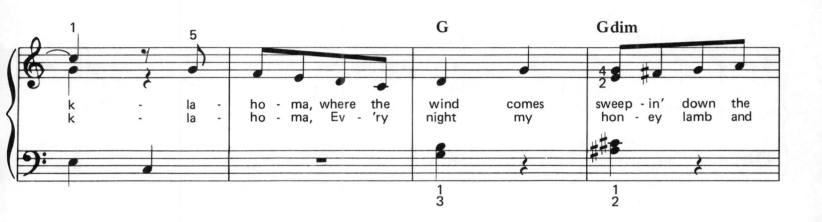

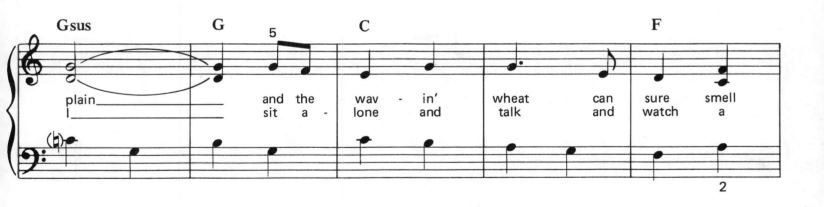

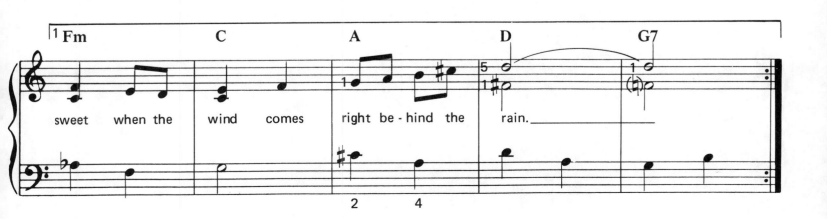

120

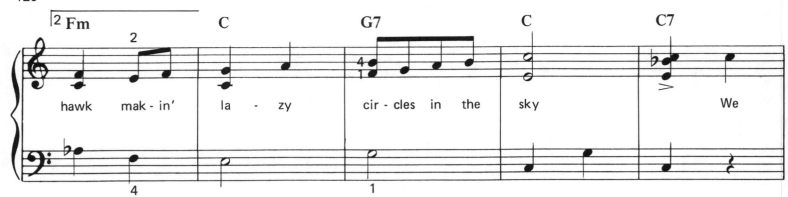

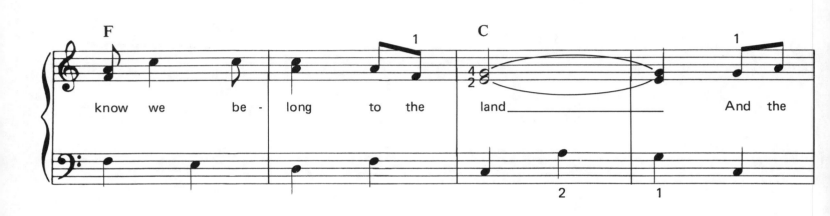

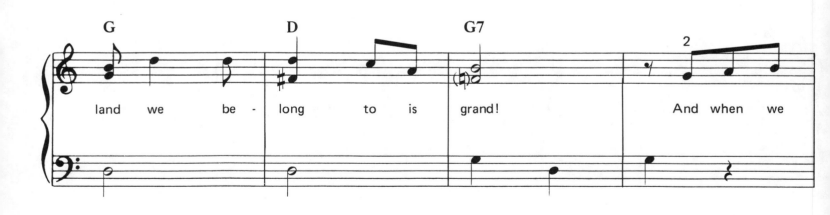

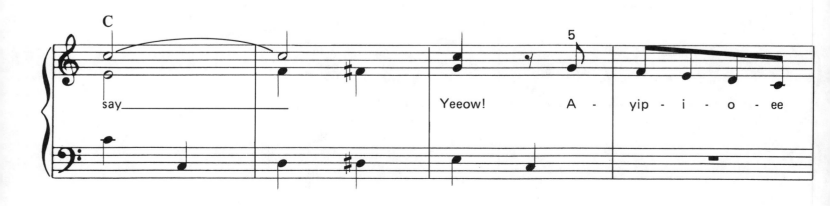

ay! _____ We're on - ly say - in'

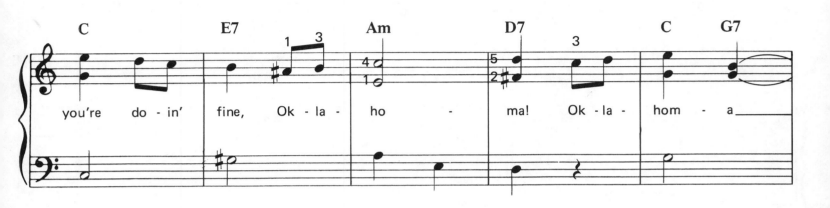

you're do - in' fine, Ok - la - ho - ma! Ok - la - hom - a ____

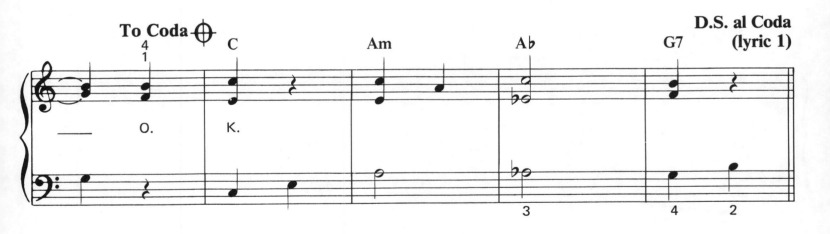

To Coda ⊕   C   Am   A♭   G7   **D.S. al Coda** (lyric 1)

__ O.   K.

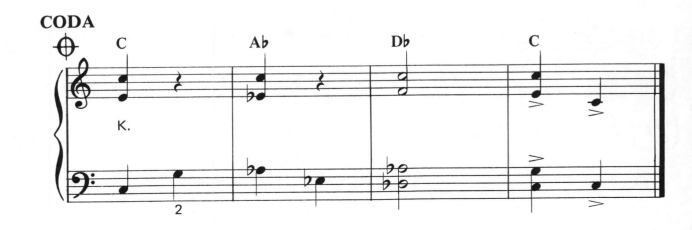

CODA ⊕   C   A♭   D♭   C

K.

A NIGHTINGALE SANG IN BERKELEY SQUARE

Lyric by ERIC MASCHWITZ
Music by MANNING SHERWIN

That cer-tain night, The night we met, There was
strange it was, How sweet and strange, There was

ma-gic a-broad in the air There were an-gels din-ing
ne-ver a dream to com-pare With that ha-zy, cra-zy

at the Ritz, And a night-in-gale sang in Ber - k'ley
night we met, When a night-in-gale sang in Ber - k'ley

124

OH, WHAT A BEAUTIFUL MORNIN'

(From "OKLAHOMA!")

Lyrics by OSCAR HAMMERSTEIN II
Music by RICHARD RODGERS

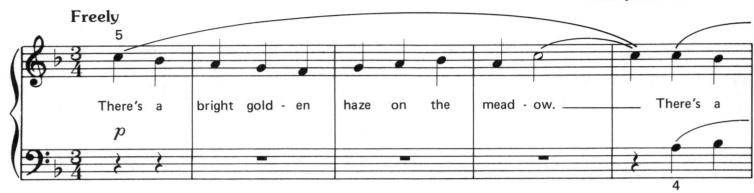

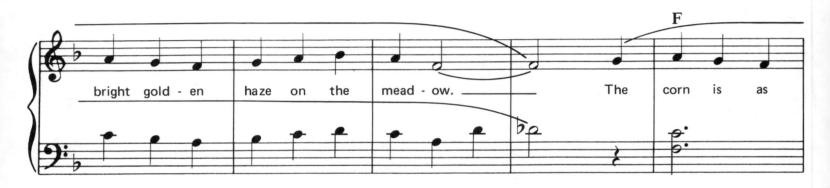

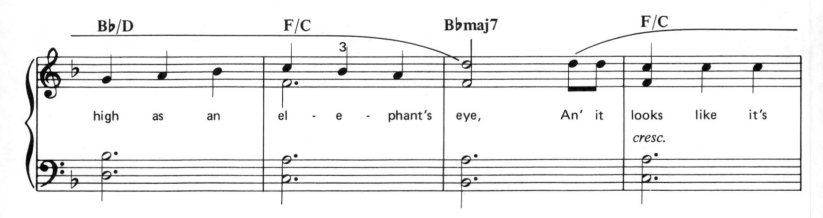

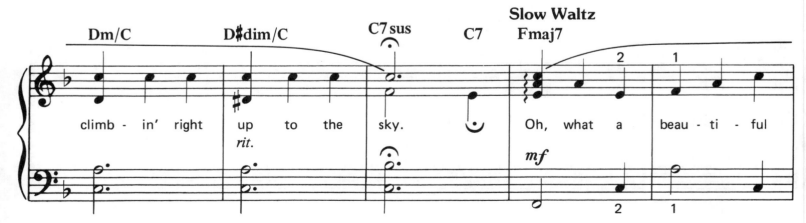

morn - in', Oh, what a beau - ti - ful

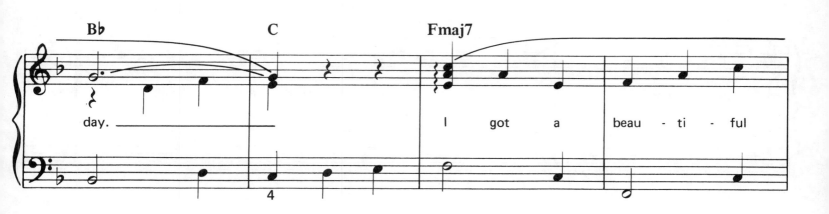

day. _____ I got a beau - ti - ful

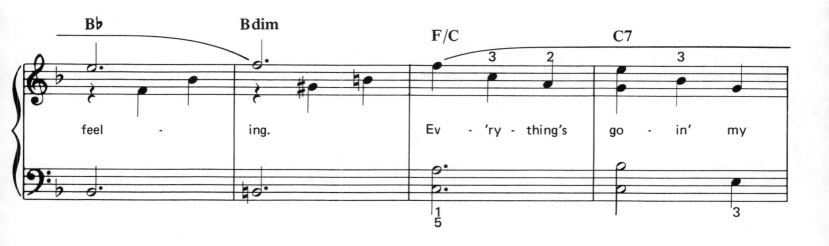

feel - ing. Ev - 'ry - thing's go - in' my

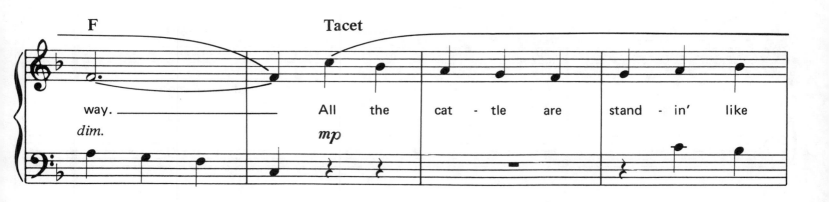

way. _____ All the cat - tle are stand - in' like

dim.　　　　mp

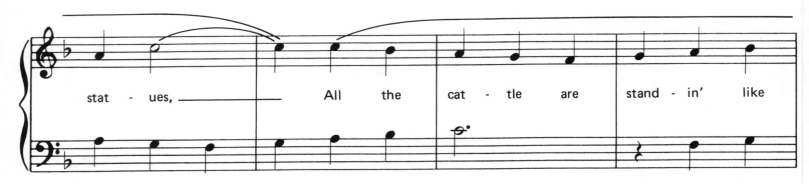

stat - ues, _____ All the cat - tle are stand - in' like

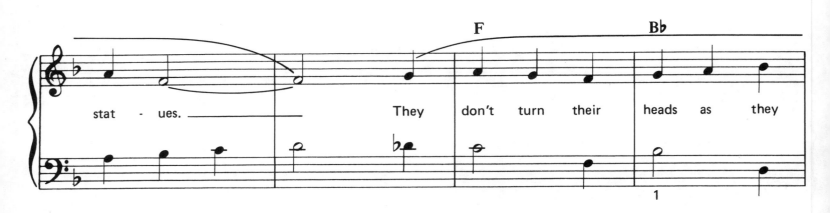

F   B♭

stat - ues. _____ They don't turn their heads as they

1

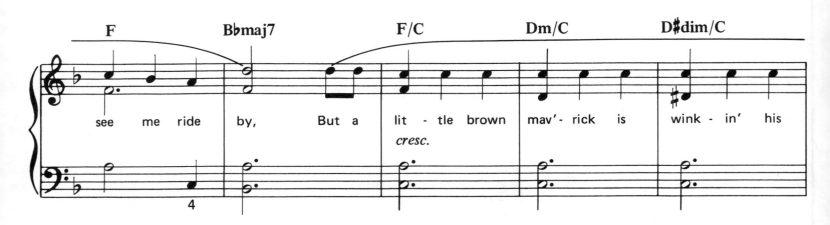

F   B♭maj7   F/C   Dm/C   D♯dim/C

see me ride by, But a lit - tle brown mav' - rick is wink - in' his
cresc.

4

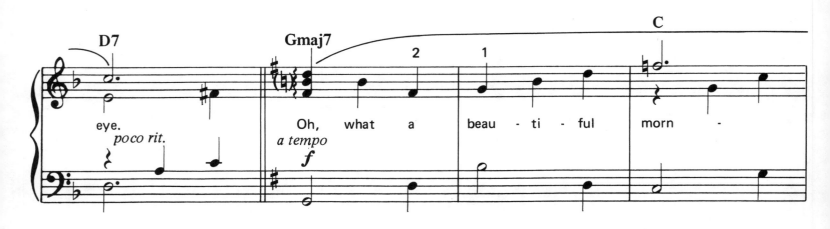

D7   Gmaj7   2   1   C

eye. Oh, what a beau - ti - ful morn -
poco rit.   a tempo
f

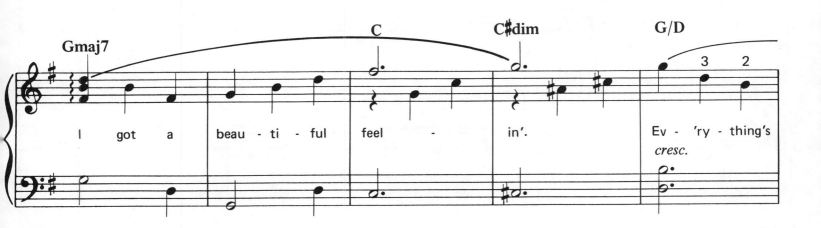

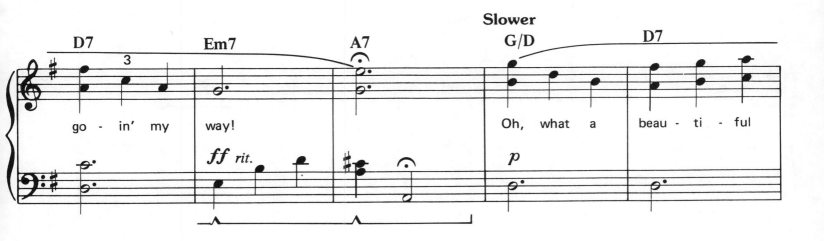

OLD DEVIL MOON
(From "FINIAN'S RAINBOW")

Words by E.Y. HARBURG
Music by BURTON LANE

Moderately

With pedal

I / You've

look at you and sud - den - ly,
got me fly - in' high and wide

some - thing in your eyes I see
On a mag - ic car - pet ride

soon be - gins be - witch - ing
Full of but - ter - flies in -

me. ____
side. ____

It's the Old Dev - il
Wan - na cry, wan - na

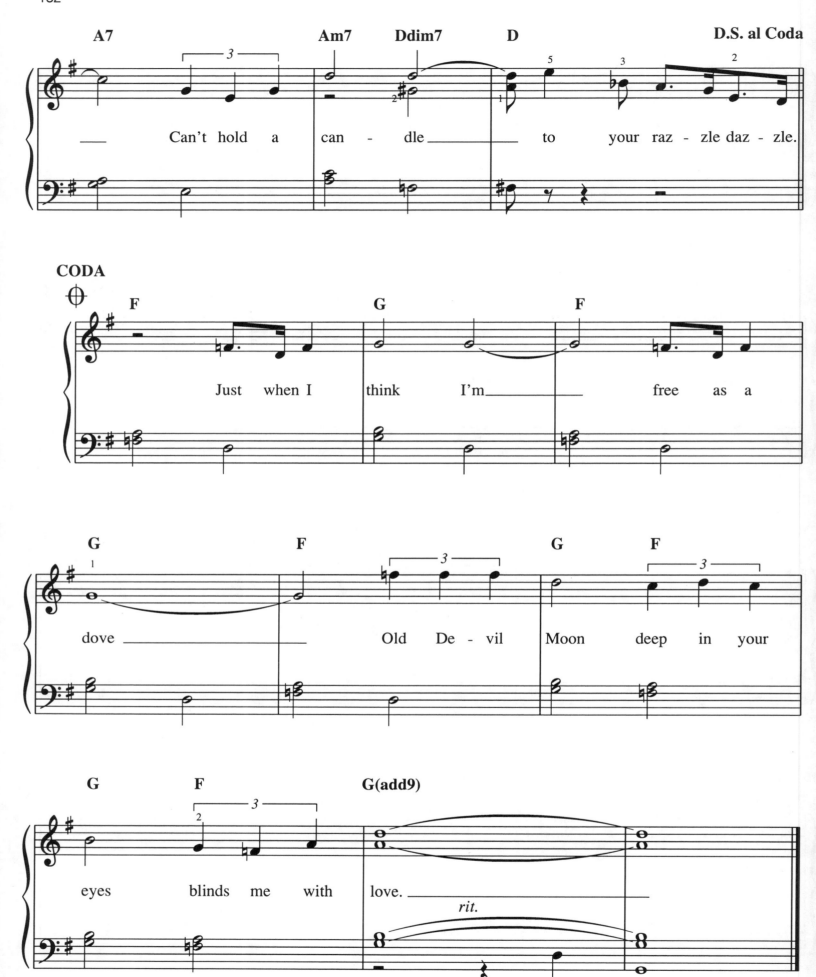

OPUS ONE

Words and Music by
SY OLIVER

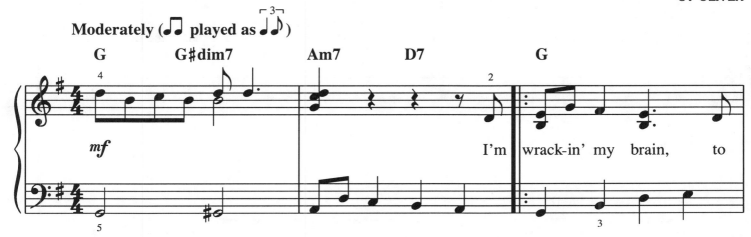

if you can swing, it's got a good beat,__ And that's the main thing, to

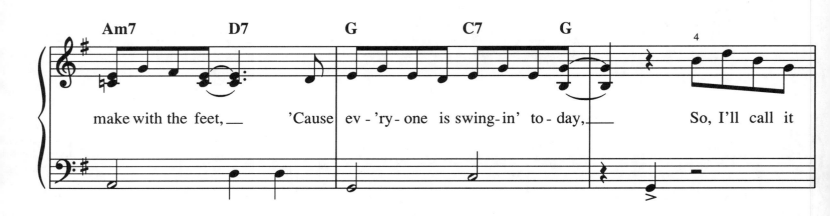

make with the feet,__ 'Cause ev-'ry-one is swing-in' to-day,__ So, I'll call it

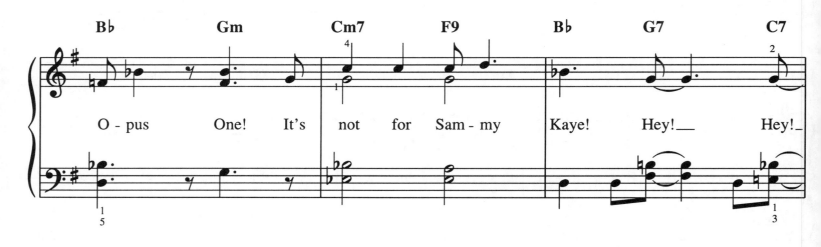

O - pus One! It's not for Sam - my Kaye! Hey!__ Hey!__

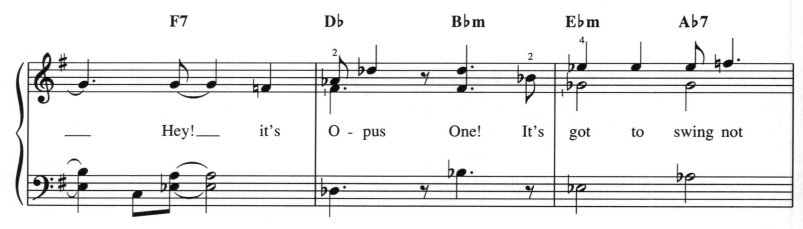

__ Hey!__ it's O - pus One! It's got to swing not

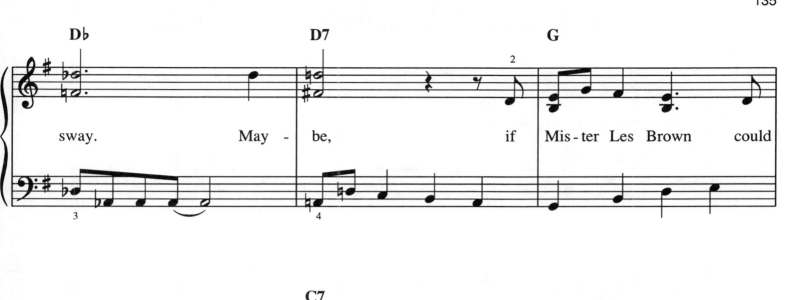

sway. May - be, if Mis - ter Les Brown could

make it re - nown __ And Ray An - tho - ny could swing it for me, __ There's

nev - er a doubt you'll knock your- self out, __ When- ev - er you can hear O - pus One. __

I'm

THE OLD LAMPLIGHTER

Words by CHARLES TOBIAS
Music by NAT SIMON

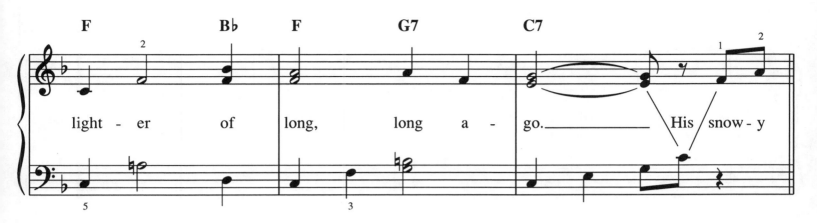

light - er of long, long a - go._____ His snow - y

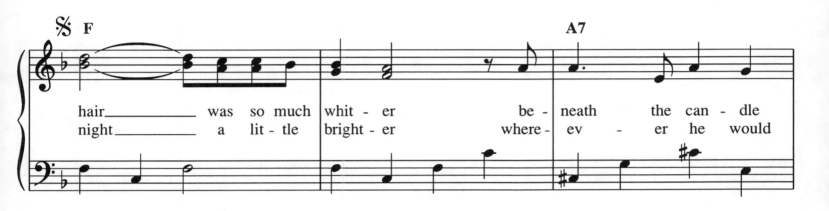

hair_____ was so much whit - er be - neath the can - dle
night_____ a lit - tle bright - er where - ev - er he would

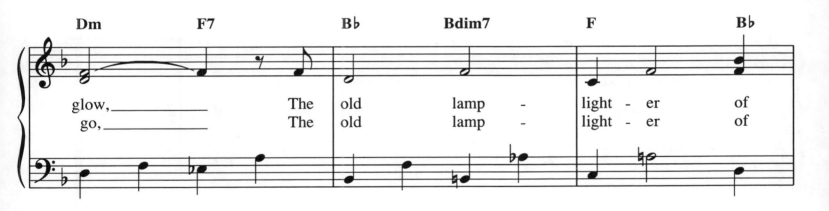

glow,_____ The old lamp - light - er of
go,_____ The old lamp - light - er of

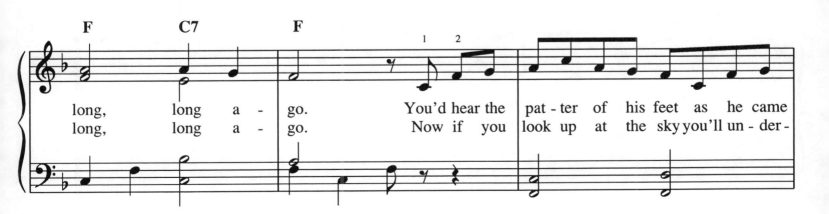

long, long a - go. You'd hear the pat - ter of his feet as he came
long, long a - go. Now if you look up at the sky you'll un - der-

To Coda ⊕

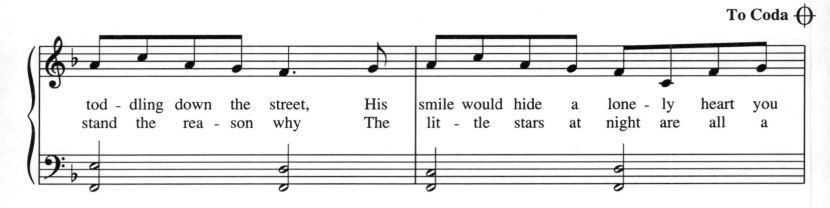

tod - dling   down   the   street,   His   smile   would   hide   a   lone - ly   heart   you
stand   the   rea - son   why   The   lit - tle   stars   at   night   are   all   a

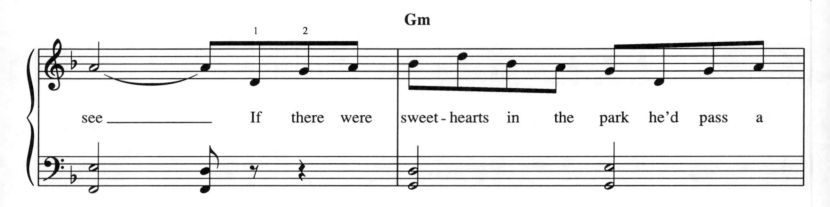

Gm

see _____ If   there   were   sweet - hearts   in   the   park   he'd   pass   a

lamp   and   leave   it   dark   Re - mem - ber - ing   the   days   that   used   to

Gm7   C7   F

be. _____ For   he   re - calls   when   dreams   were   new,   he   loved   some -

THE OLD SOFT SHOE

Words by NANCY HAMILTON
Music by MORGAN LEWIS

was - n't a num - ber sug - gest - ing a rhum - ba on all the bill,___ And

as for the Con - ga of Ma - dame Li - zon - ga it just was nil.___ They'd

all of them paid and the bal - co - ny trade would - n't leave their seats___ un - til

We gave them the Old Soft Shoe! Danc - es come, danc - es go like the

PEOPLE WILL SAY WE'RE IN LOVE
(From "OKLAHOMA!")

Lyrics by OSCAR HAMMERSTEIN II
Music by RICHARD RODGERS

With a lilt

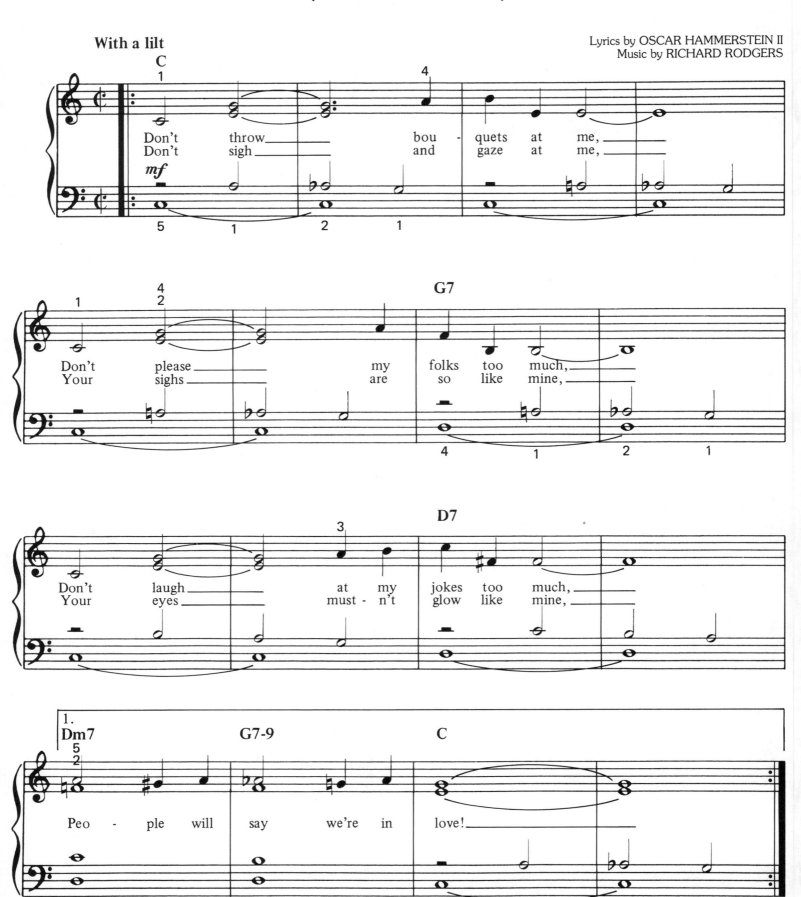

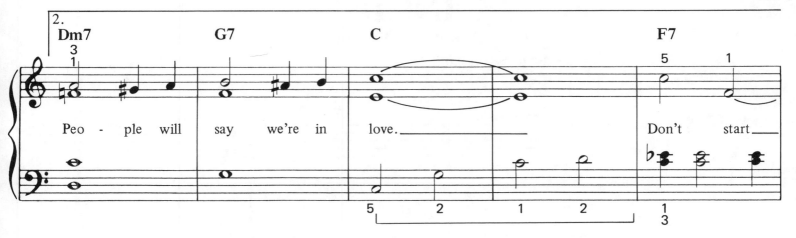

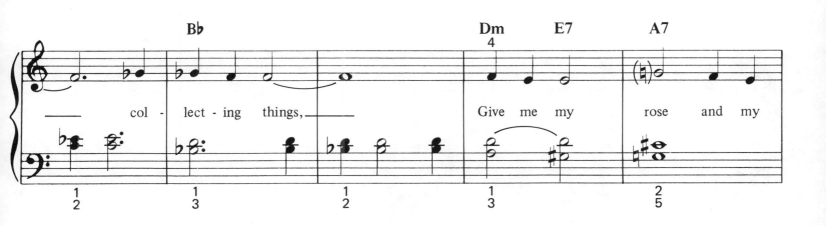

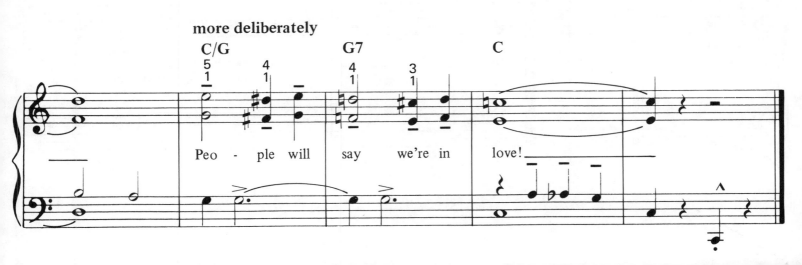

POINCIANA
(Song Of The Tree)

Moderately Slow Beguine tempo

Words by BUDDY BERNIER
Music by NAT SIMON

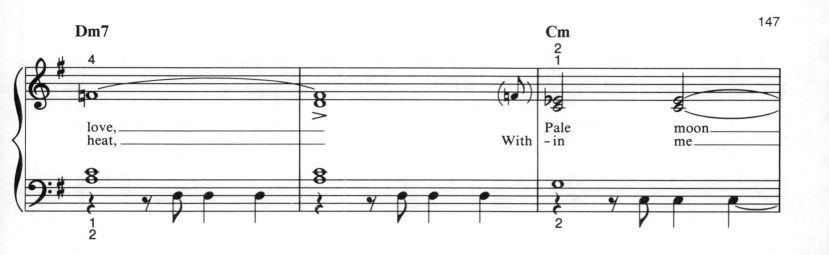

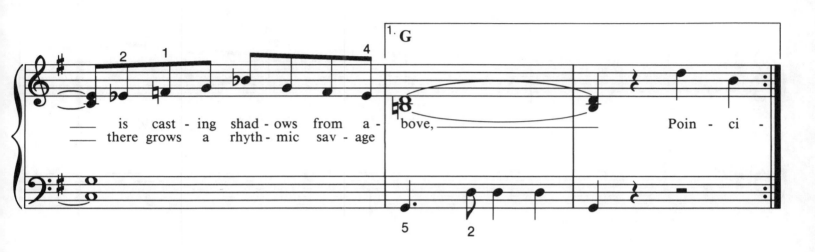

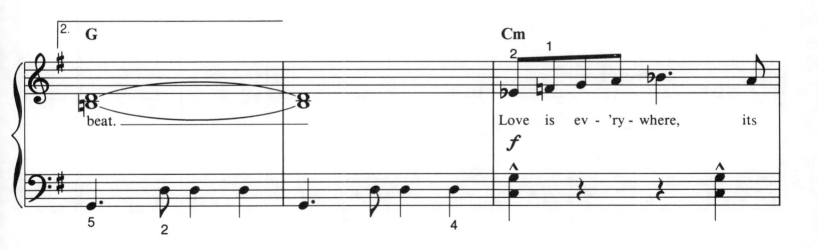

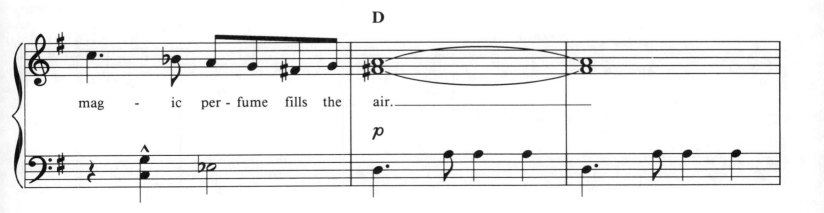

To and fro you sway, my heart's in time, I've learned to care.

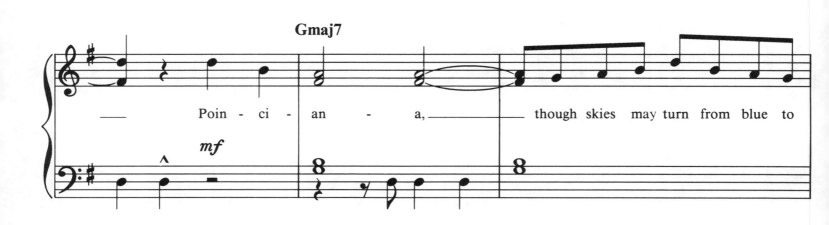

Poin - ci - an - a, though skies may turn from blue to

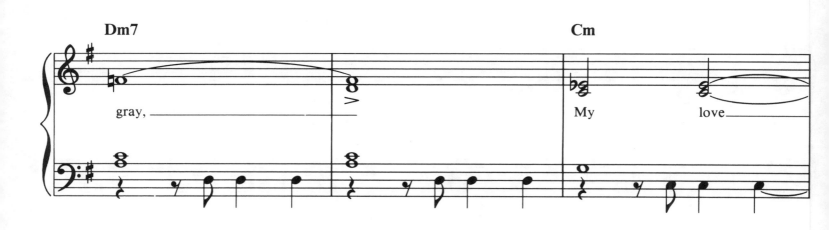

gray, My love

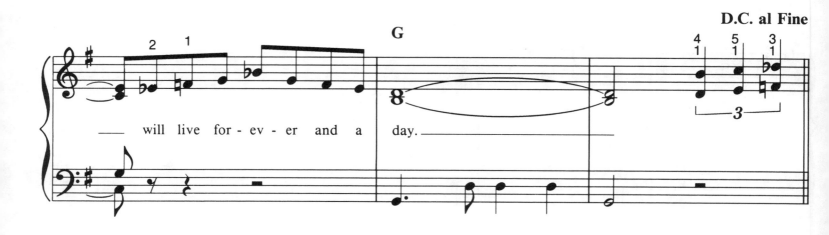

will live for - ev - er and a day.

RED ROSES FOR A BLUE LADY

Words and Music by SID TEPPER
and ROY C. BENNETT

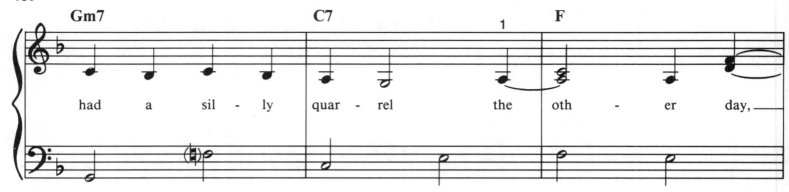

had a sil - ly quar - rel the oth - er day, ___

___ Hope these pret - ty flow - ers chase her

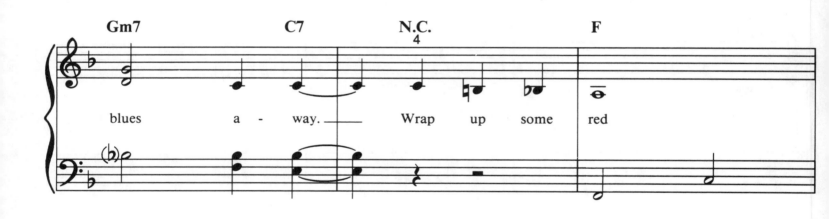

blues a - way. ___ Wrap up some red

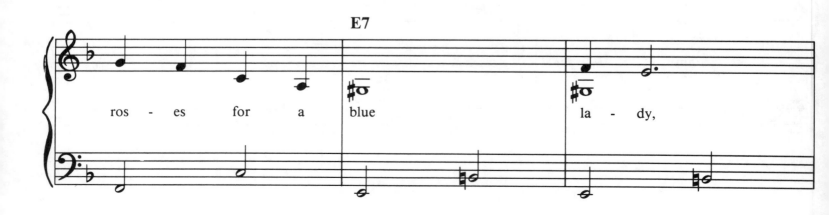

ros - es for a blue la - dy,

Send them to the sweet - est gal in town, _____

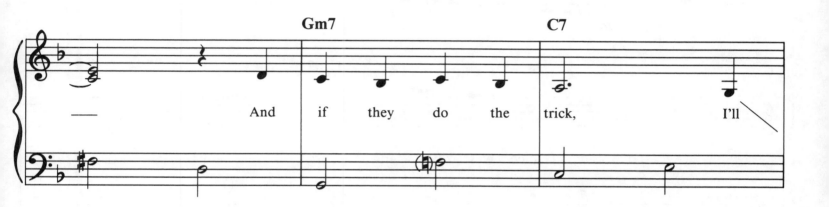

_____ And if they do the trick, I'll

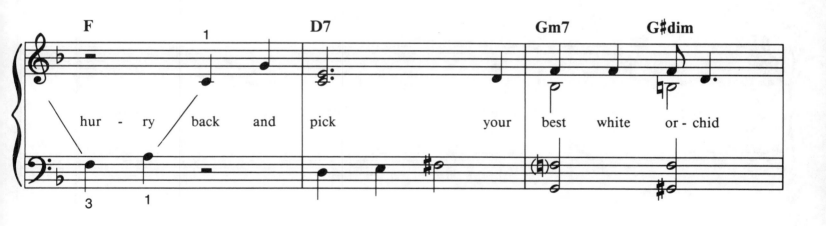

hur - ry back and pick your best white or - chid

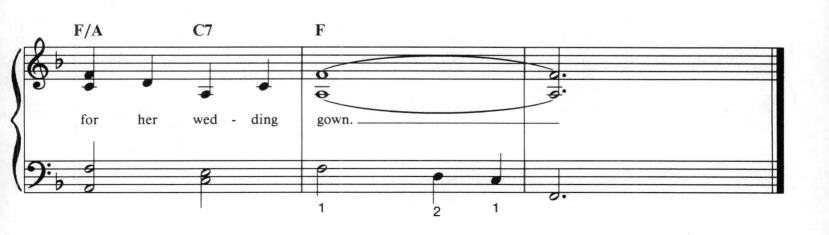

for her wed - ding gown. _____

POLKA DOTS AND MOONBEAMS

Words by JOHNNY BURKE
Music by JIMMY VAN HEUSEN

A coun-try dance was be-ing held in a gar-den,

I felt a bump and heard an "Oh, beg your par-don,"

Sud-den-ly I saw Pol-ka Dots And Moon-beams All a-round a pug-nosed

SATURDAY NIGHT IS THE LONELIEST NIGHT OF THE WEEK

Words by SAMMY CAHN
Music by JULE STYNE

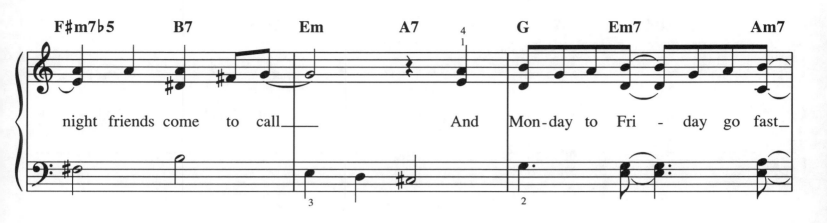

night friends come to call____ And Mon-day to Fri - day go fast__

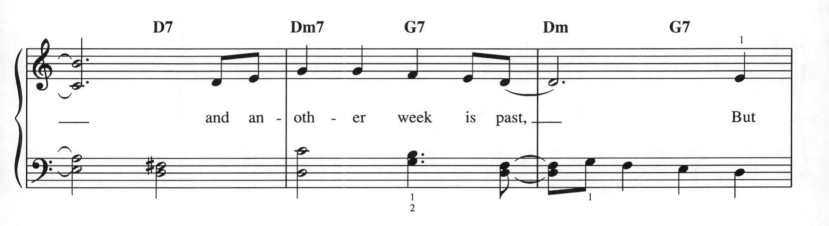

____ and an - oth - er week is past,____ But

Sat - ur - day Night _ is the lone - li - est night _ in the week,_____

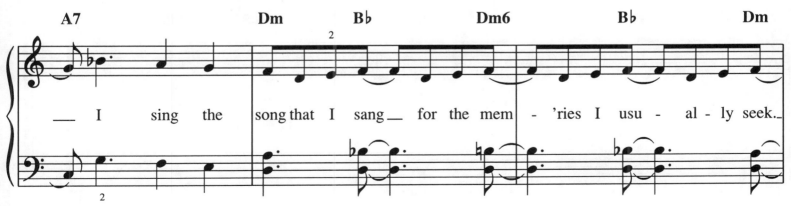

__ I sing the song that I sang__ for the mem - 'ries I usu - al - ly seek._

SEEMS LIKE OLD TIMES

Words and Music by JOHN JACOB LOEB
and CARMEN LOMBARDO

SHOO FLY PIE
AND APPLE PAN DOWDY

Words by SAMMY GALLOP
Music by GUY WOOD

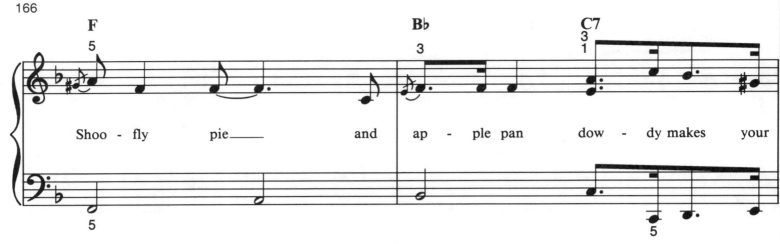

Shoo - fly pie___ and ap - ple pan dow - dy makes your

eyes light up,___ your tum - my say "how - dy," Shoo - fly pie___ and

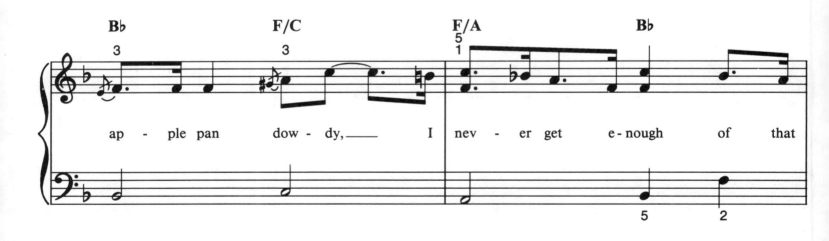

ap - ple pan dow - dy,___ I nev - er get e - nough of that

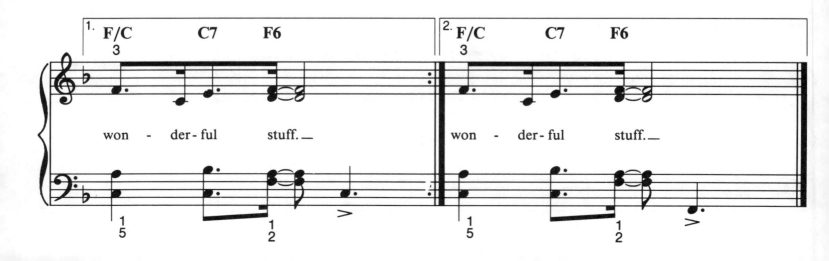

1. won - der - ful stuff.___

2. won - der - ful stuff.___

SO IN LOVE
(From "KISS ME KATE")

Words and Music by COLE PORTER

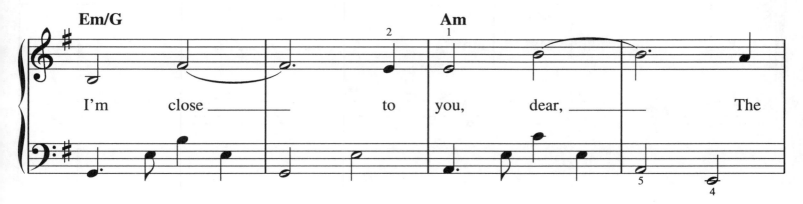

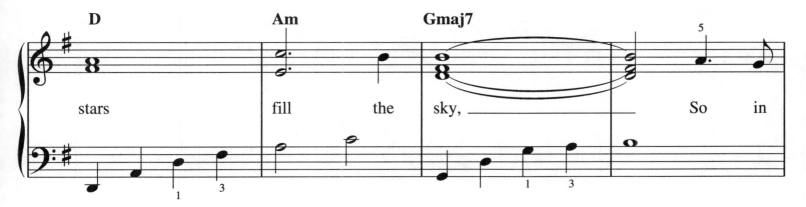

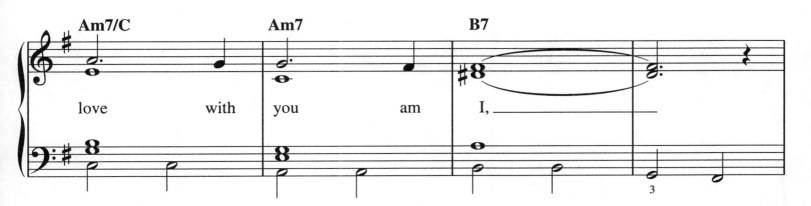

E - ven, _____ with - out you, _____

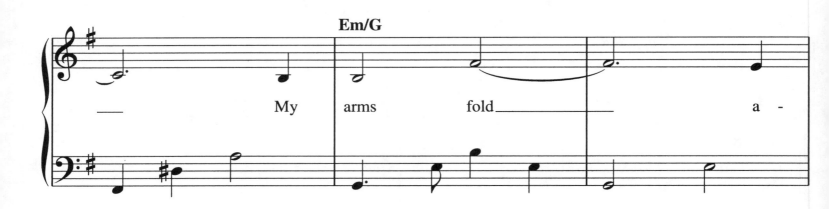

___ My arms fold_____ a -

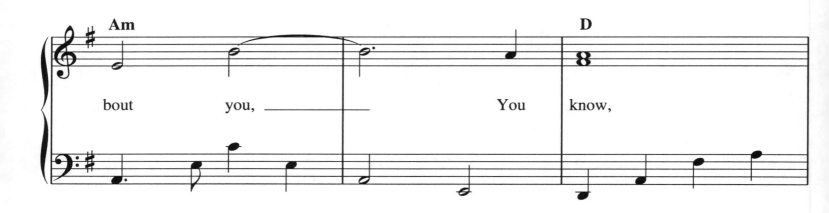

bout you, _____ You know,

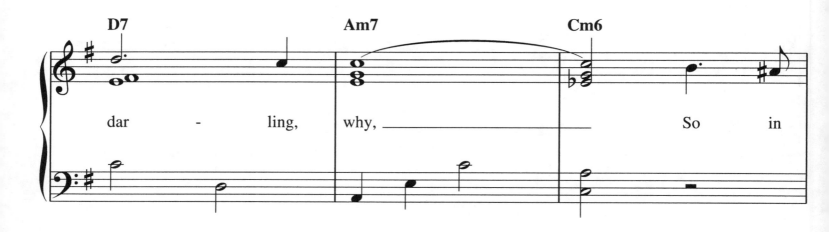

dar - ling, why, _____ So in

love _____ with you am I. _____

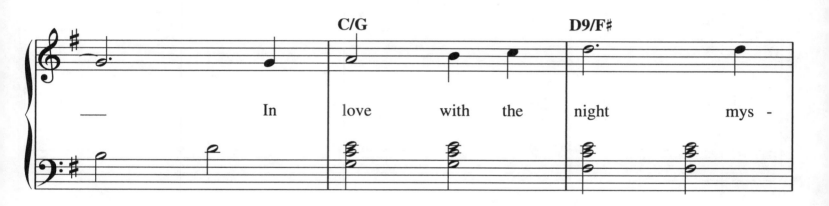

___ In love with the night mys -

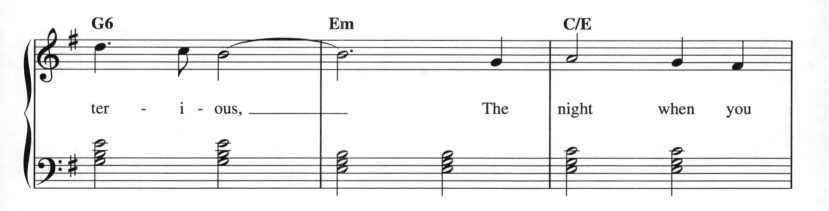

ter - i - ous, _____ The night when you

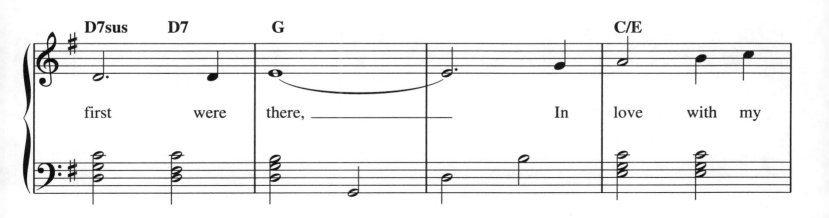

first were there, _____ In love with my

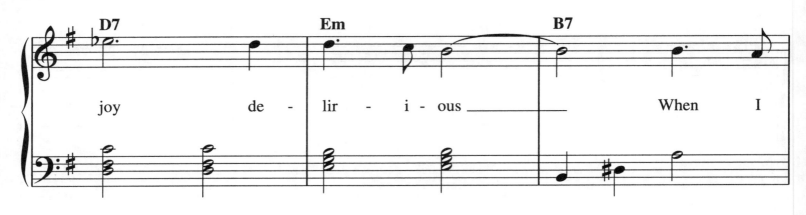

joy de - lir - i - ous _____ When I

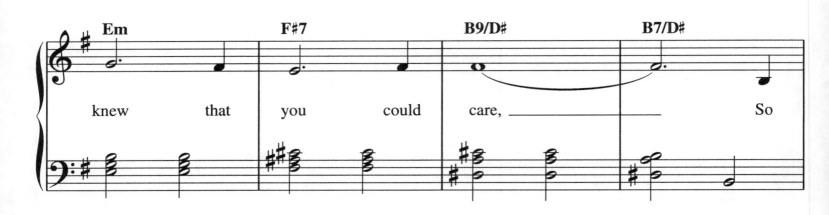

knew that you could care, _____ So

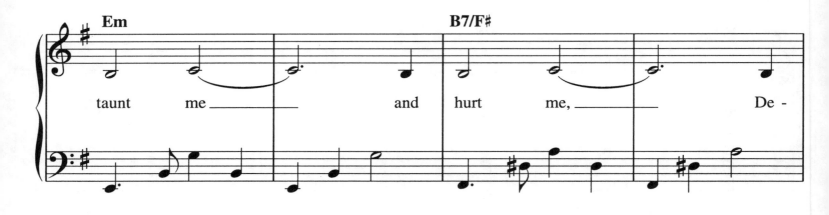

taunt me _____ and hurt me, _____ De -

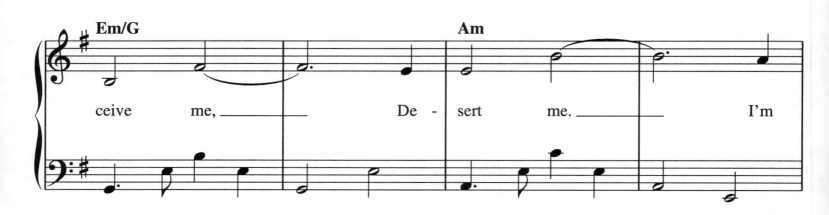

ceive me, _____ De - sert me. _____ I'm

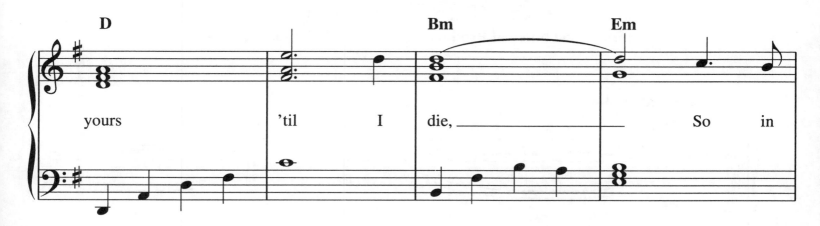

yours   'til   I   die, _____   So   in

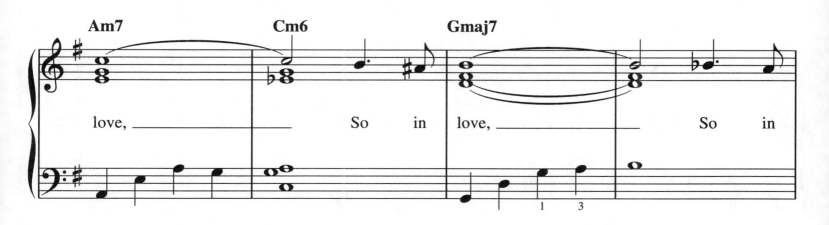

love, _____   So   in   love, _____   So   in

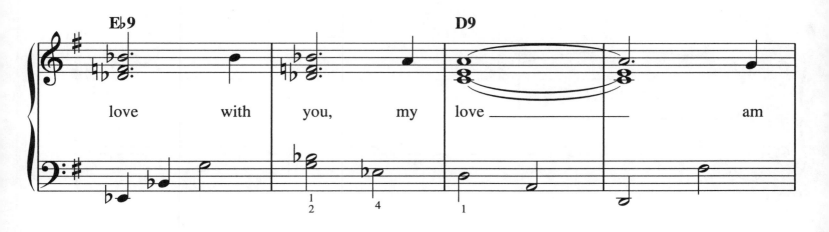

love   with   you,   my   love _____   am

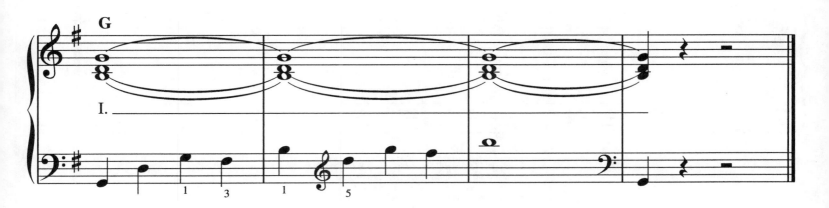

I. _____

SPEAK LOW

(From The Musical Production "ONE TOUCH OF VENUS")

Words by OGDEN NASH
Music by KURT WEILL

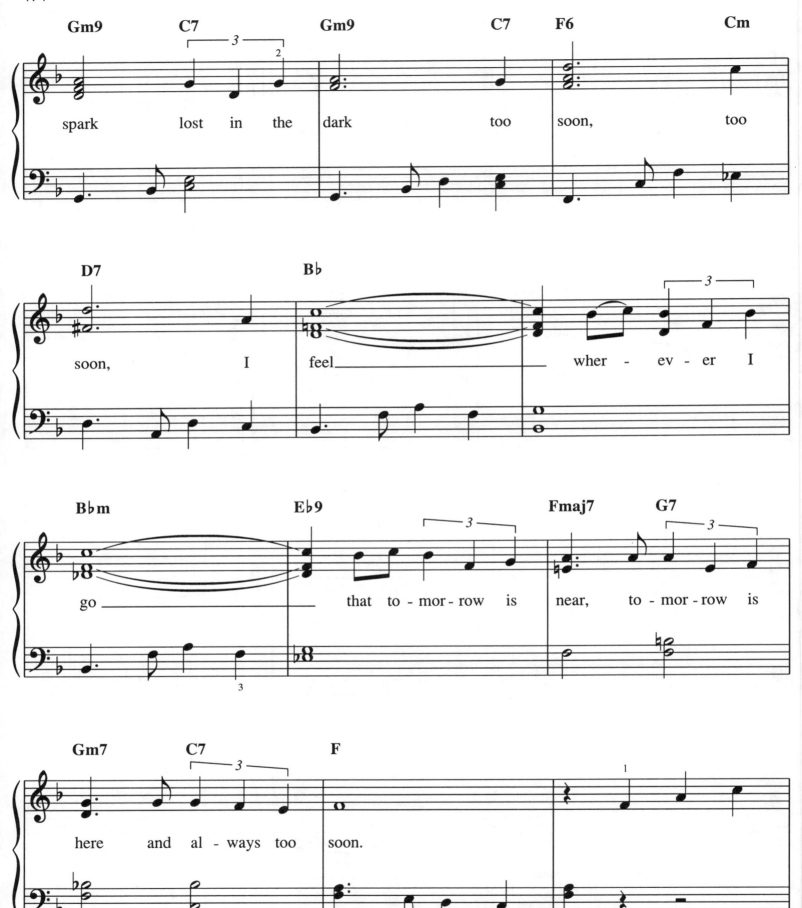

THE SURREY WITH THE FRINGE ON TOP
(From "OKLAHOMA!")

Lyrics by OSCAR HAMMERSTEIN II
Music by RICHARD RODGERS

Easily, with a bounce

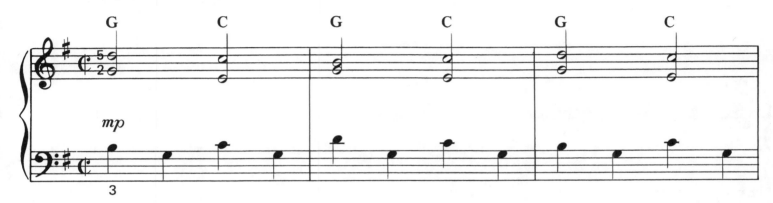

When I take you out to-night with

me _____   Hon - ey here's the

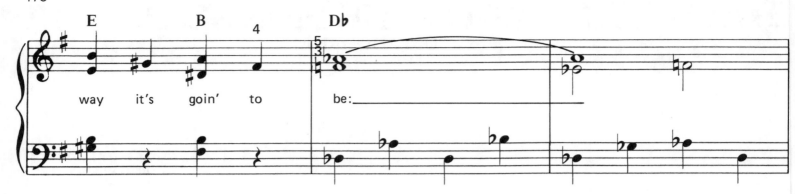

way it's goin' to be:_____

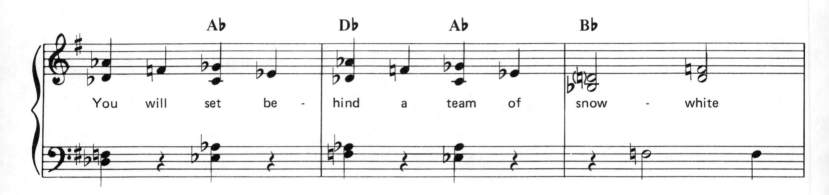

You will set be - hind a team of snow - white

hors - es, in the slick - est gig you ev - er

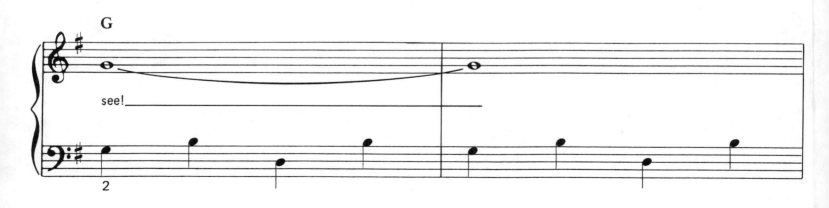

see!_____

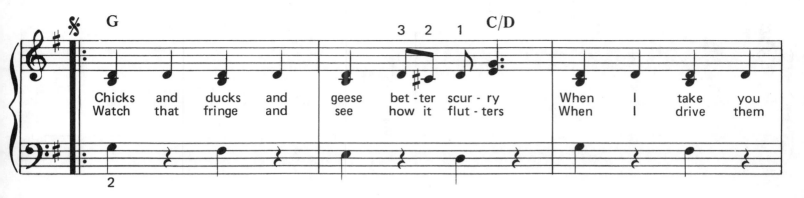

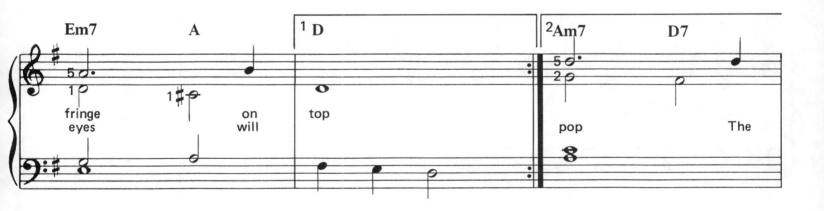

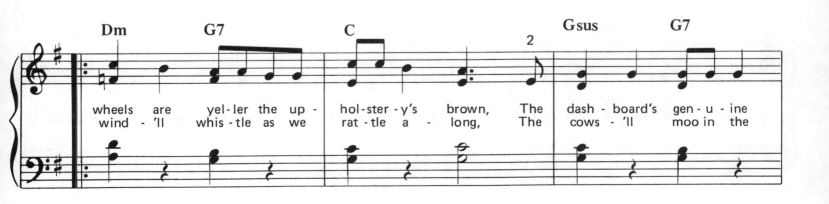

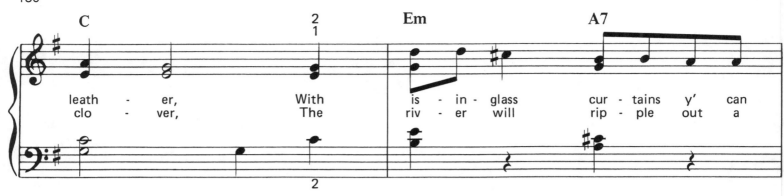

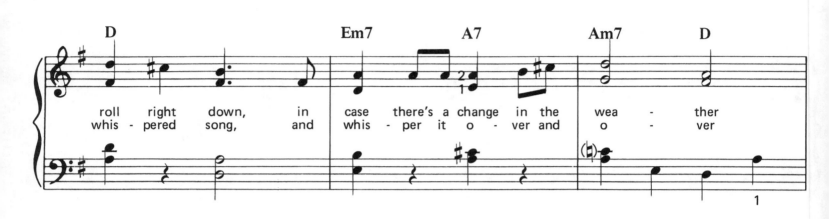

Keer - to swap Fer that shin - y lit - tle sur - rey with the
nev - er stop In that shin - y lit - tle sur - rey with the

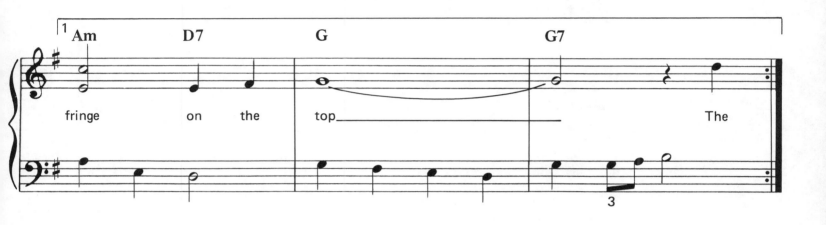

fringe on the top_____ The

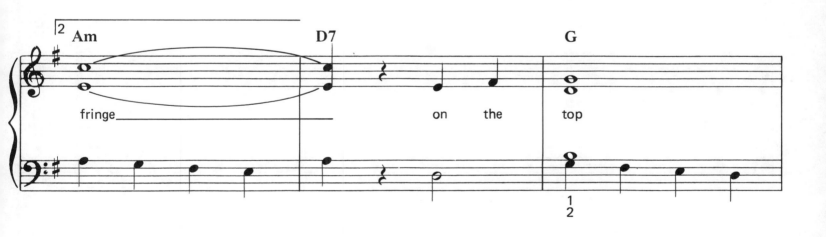

fringe_____ on the top

A STRING OF PEARLS

Words by EDDIE DeLANGE
Music by JERRY GRAY

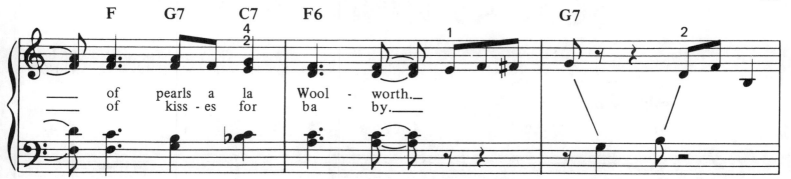

of pearls a la Wool - worth.
of kiss - es for ba - by.

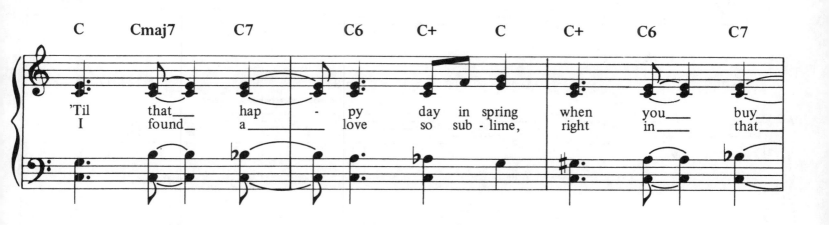

'Til that__ hap - py day in spring when you__ buy__
I found__ a__ love so sub - lime, right in__ that__

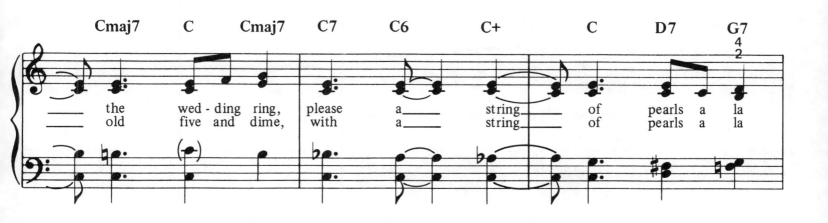

the wed - ding ring, please a__ string__ of pearls a la
old five and dime, with a__ string__ of pearls a la

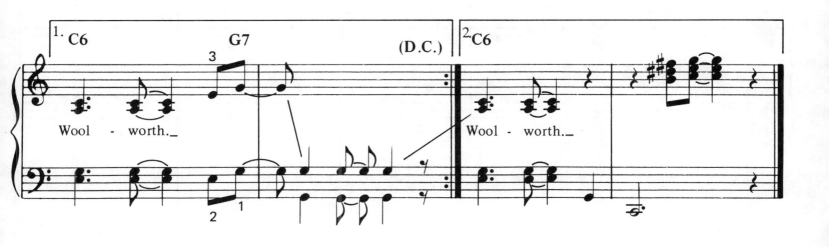

Wool - worth.__ (D.C.) Wool - worth.__

A SUNDAY KIND OF LOVE

Words and Music by BARBARA BELLE,
LOUIS PRIMA, ANITA LEONARD and STAN RHODES

MCA music publishing

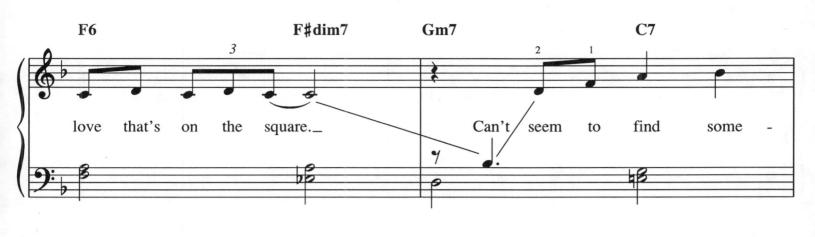

love that's on the square.___ Can't seem to find some -

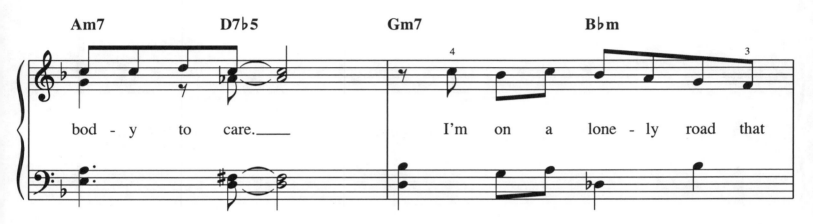

bod - y to care.___ I'm on a lone - ly road that

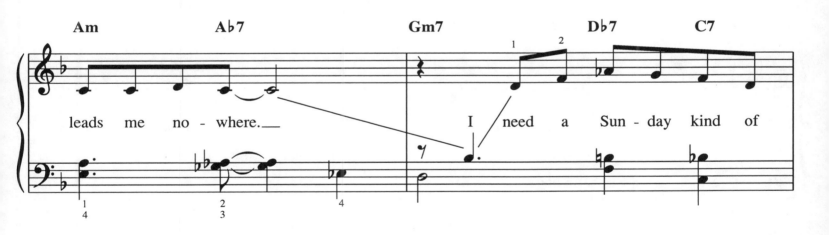

leads me no - where.___ I need a Sun - day kind of

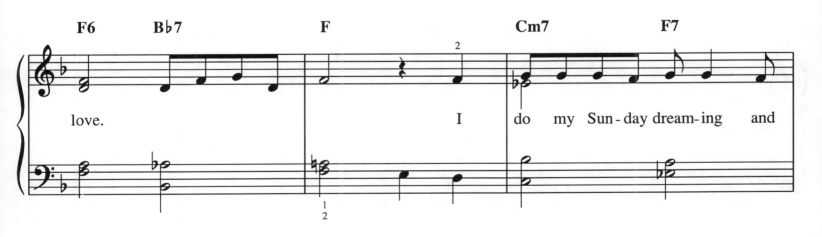

love. I do my Sun - day dream - ing and

SWINGIN' ON A STAR

Words by JOHNNY BURKE
Music by JIMMY VAN HEUSEN

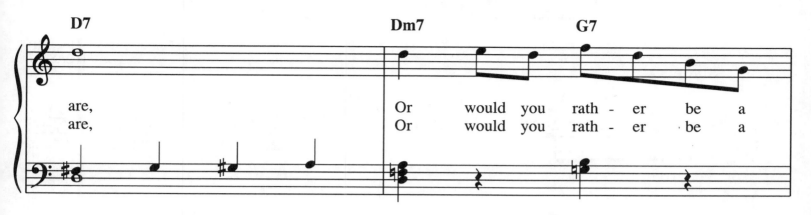

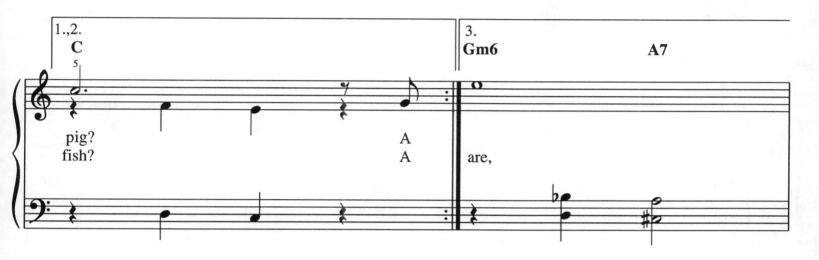

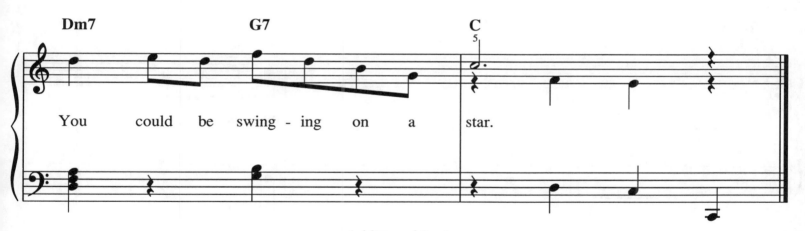

Additional Lyrics

A fish won't do anything but swim in a brook,
He can't write his name or read a book.
To fool the people is his only thought
And though he's slippery, he still gets caught,
But then if that sort of life is what you wish,
You may grow up to be a fish.

And all the monkeys aren't in the zoo,
Ev'ry day you meet quite a few,
So you see it's all up to you.
You can be better than you are.
You could be swinging on a star.

THERE MUST BE A WAY

Words and Music by SAMMY GALLOP
and DAVID SAXON

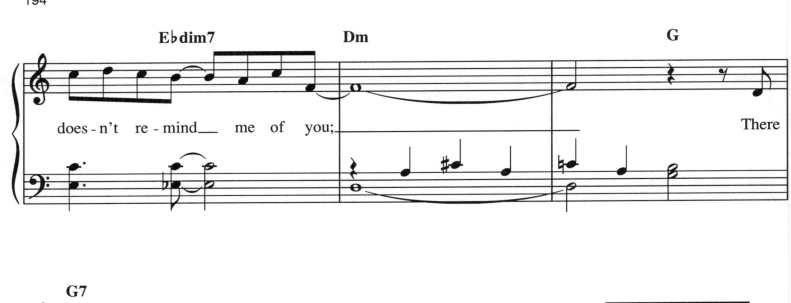

doesn't re-mind me of you; There

must be a kiss To thrill me like yours used to do.

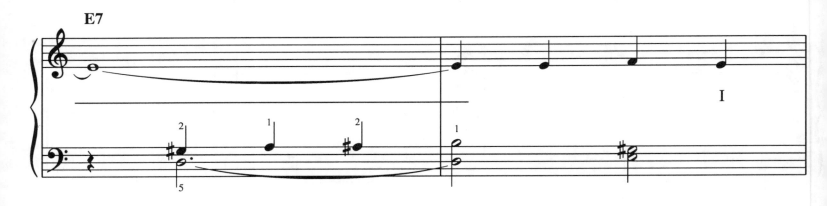

I

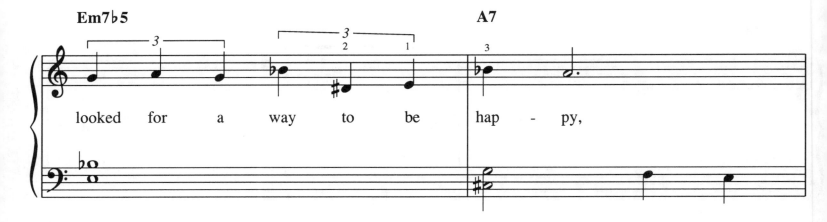

looked for a way to be hap - py,

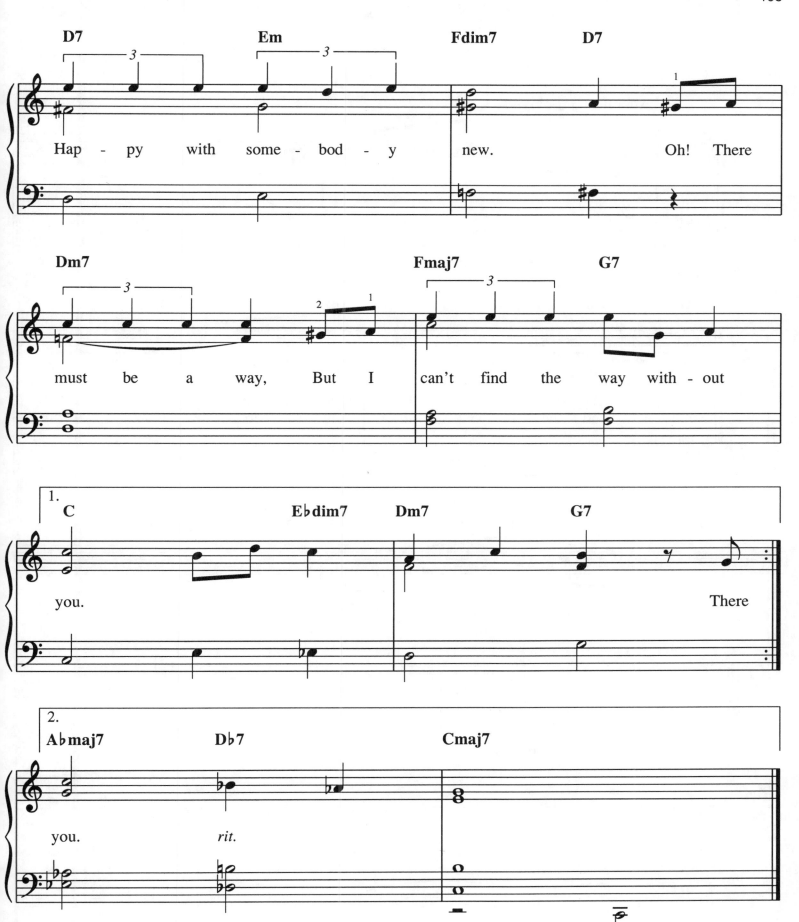

THE THINGS WE DID LAST SUMMER

Words and Music by SAMMY CAHN
and JULE STYNE

TUXEDO JUNCTION

Words by BUDDY FEYNE
Music by ERSKINE HAWKINS,
WILLIAM JOHNSON and JULIAN DASH

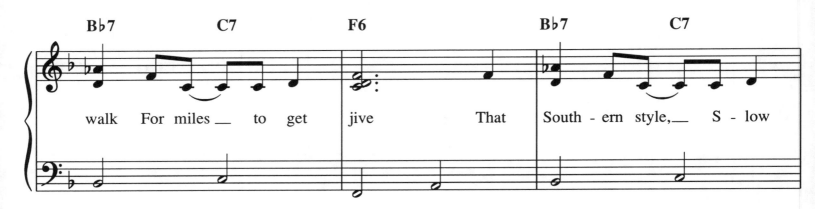

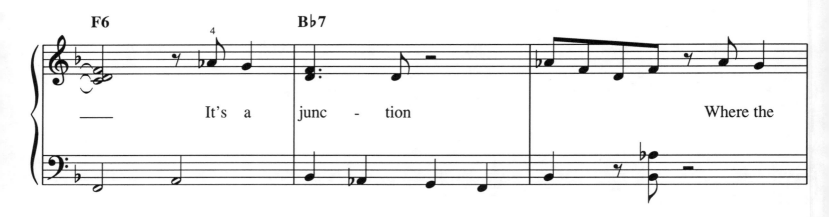

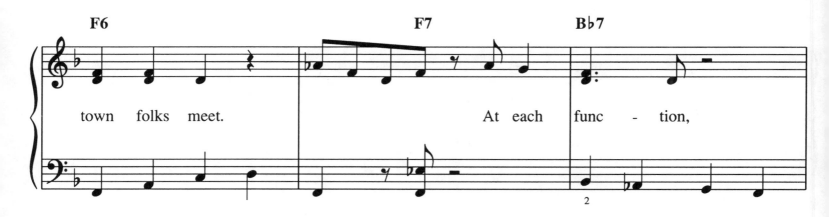

In their tux they greet you. Come on

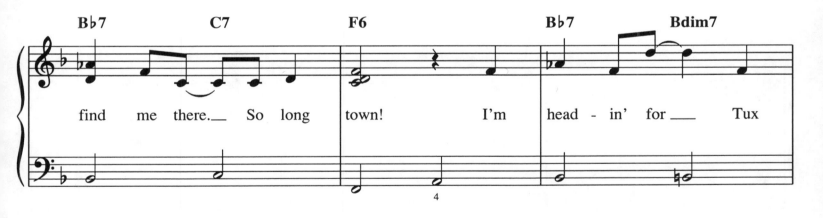

down, For - get your care. ___ Come on down You'll

find me there. ___ So long town! I'm head - in' for ___ Tux

e - do Junc - tion now. ___ Way down ___

THE THIRD MAN THEME

Words by WALTER LORD
Based on music composed
and arranged by ANTON KARAS

gleam   or a half - for - got - ten dream,

Seems to glim- mer when   you hear The Third   Man   Theme.

Once a - gain____ there comes to mind

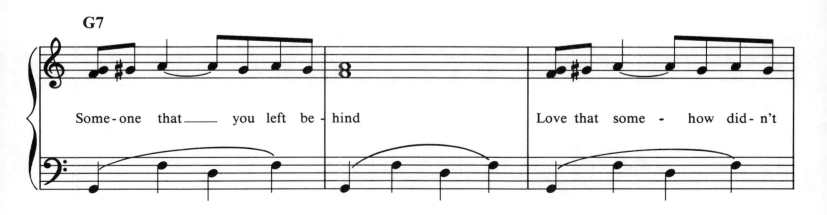

Some - one that____ you left be - hind   Love that some - how did - n't

last in that hap - py ci - ty of the past.

Does she still re - call the dream, that rap - ture so su - preme When

first she heard ___ the haunt - ing Third Man Theme? ___

Car - ni - vals and car - ou - sels and fer - ris wheels and par - a - sols. The

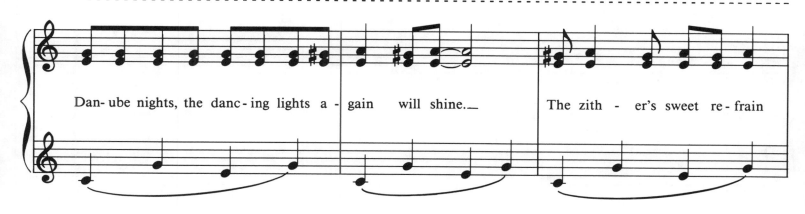

Dan-ube nights, the danc-ing lights a - gain will shine.__ The zith - er's sweet re-frain

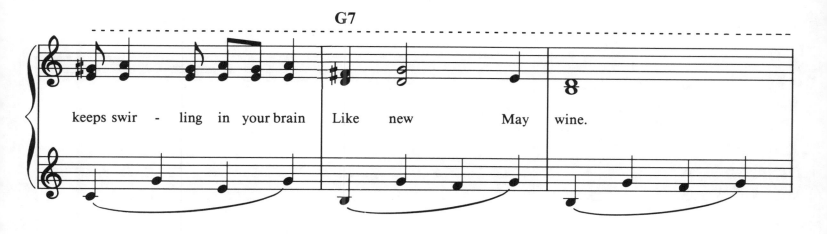

G7

keeps swir - ling in your brain Like new May wine.

Strauss waltz - es can - dle glow, __ and the laugh - ter of

long a - go ___ Fill the mag - ic clouds and make it seem like to -

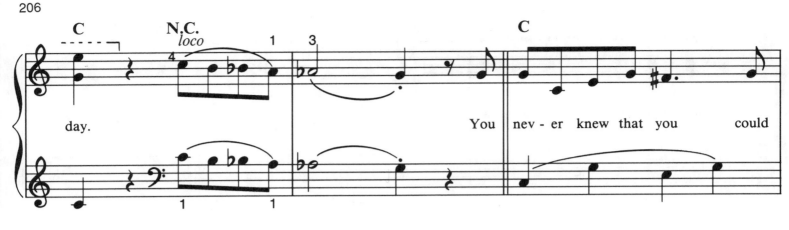

day.

You nev-er knew that you could

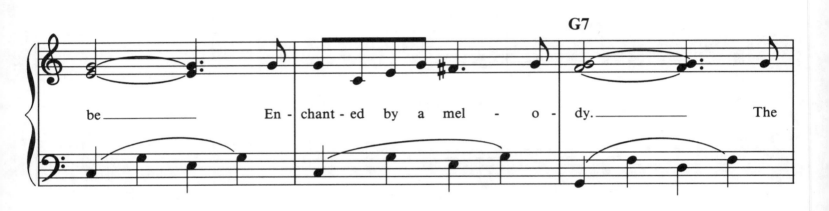

be _____ En-chant-ed by a mel-o-dy. _____ The

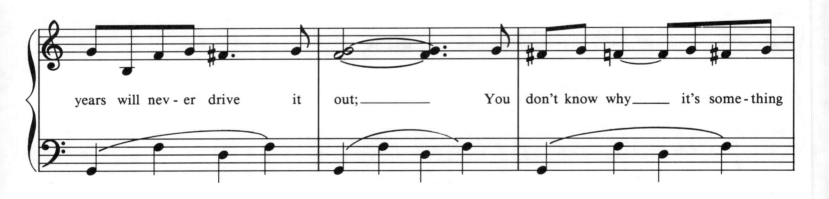

years will nev-er drive it out; _____ You don't know why _____ it's some-thing

you can live with-out. You hear it in the twi-light hush _____ And

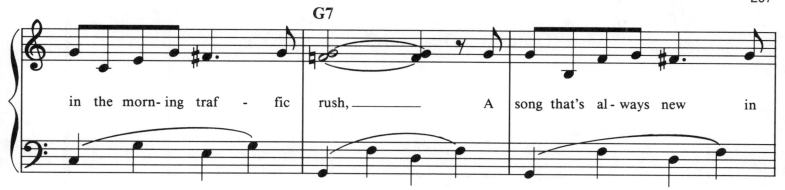

in the morn-ing traf - fic rush, _____ A song that's al-ways new in

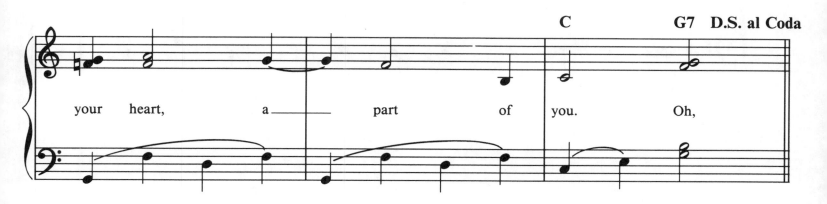

your heart, a _____ part of you. Oh,

CODA

of a well ___ re - mem- bered dream Shines so bright- ly when you

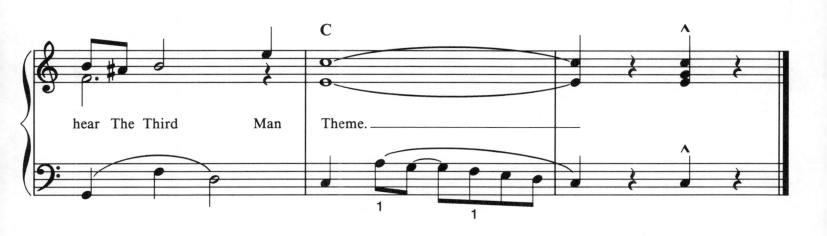

hear The Third Man Theme. _____

WHEN YOU WISH UPON A STAR
(From Walt Disney's "PINOCCHIO")

Words by NED WASHINGTON
Music by LEIGH HARLINE

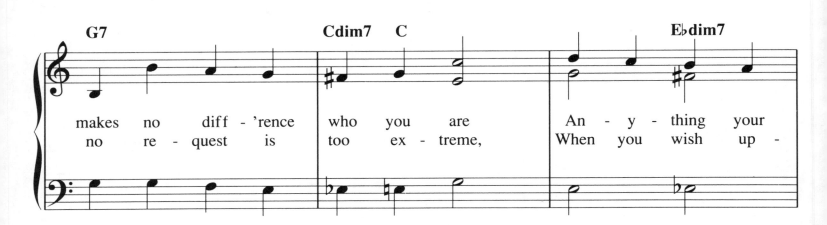

heart de - sires will / on a star as come to / dream - ers you. ____

do. Fate is kind,

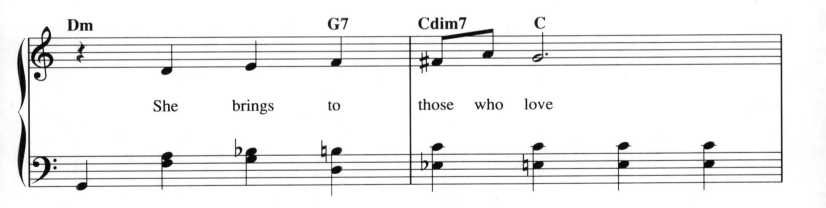

She brings to those who love

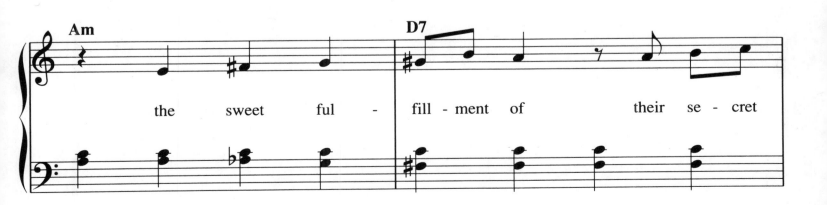

the sweet ful - fill - ment of their se - cret

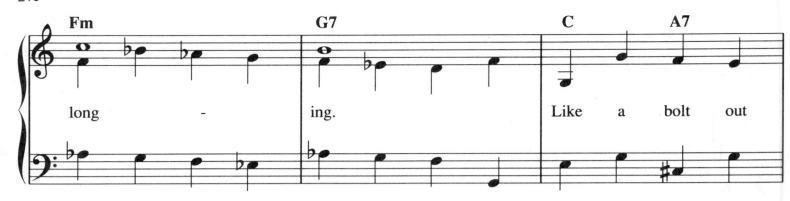

long - ing. Like a bolt out

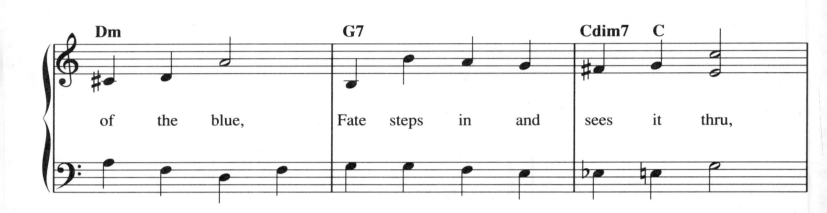

of the blue, Fate steps in and sees it thru,

When you wish up - on a star your dream comes

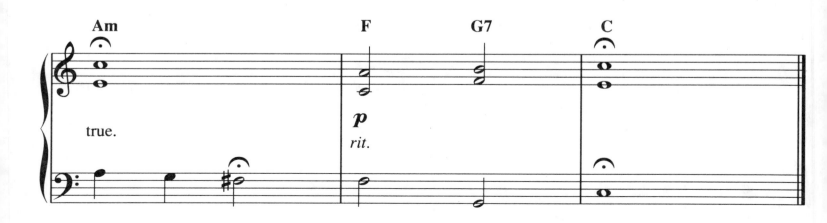

true.

WUNDERBAR
(From "KISS ME KATE")

Words and Music by COLE PORTER

YOU CAN'T BE TRUE DEAR
(Du Kannst Nicht Treu Sein)

English lyric by HAL COTTON
Original German text by GERHARD EBELER
Music by HANS OTTEN and KEN GRIFFIN

YOU'LL NEVER WALK ALONE
(From "CAROUSEL")

Lyrics by OSCAR HAMMERSTEIN II
Music by RICHARD RODGERS

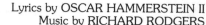

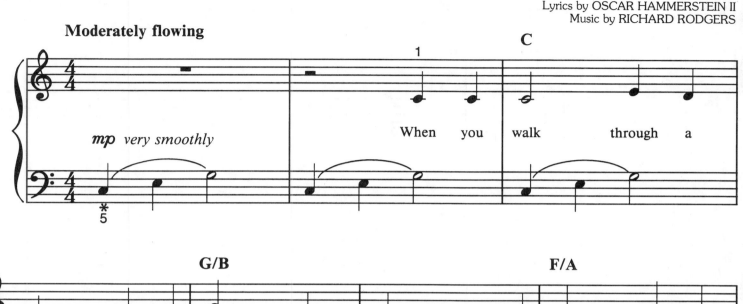

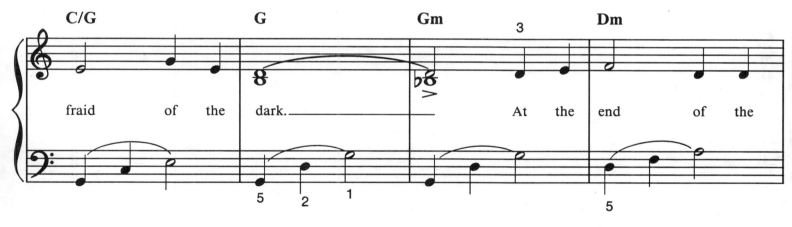

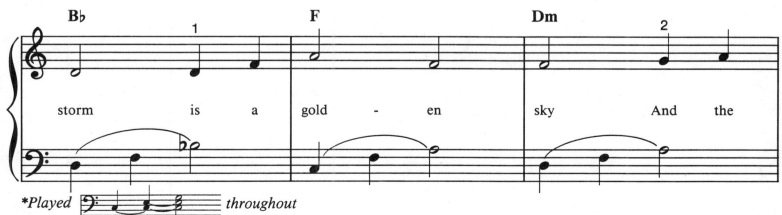

220

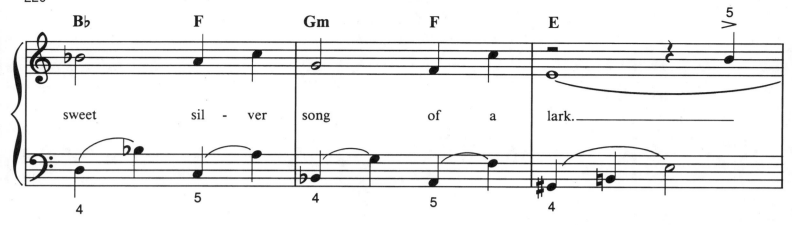

sweet   sil - ver   song   of   a   lark._____

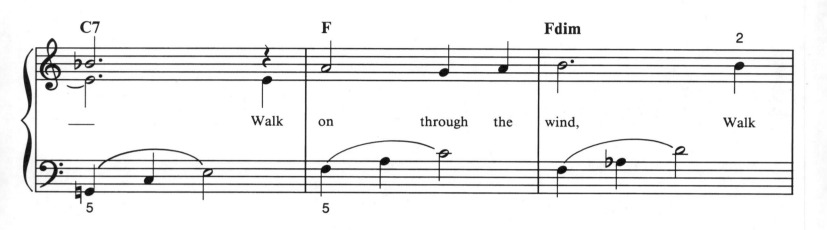

_____   Walk   on   through   the   wind,   Walk

on   through   the   rain,   Tho'   your   dreams   be

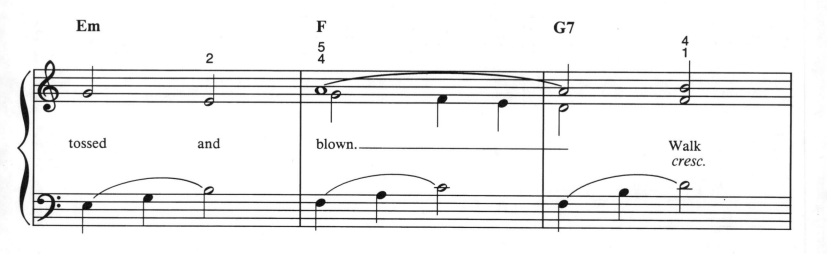

tossed   and   blown._____   Walk   *cresc.*